I0091755

The Commonwealth and Britain

First Published in 1988, *The Commonwealth and Britain* reexamines the Commonwealth connection from the perspective of British interests and priorities and assesses the need for changes in British policy. It raises questions like: Is the Commonwealth an asset or a liability to Britain in terms of international influence and obligations? Has the South African issue now become the central focus for Commonwealth consultation and conflict, or are there broader, long-term issues for which the Commonwealth remains an appropriate forum? And how useful and important for Britain are the social, cultural, and economic links which the Commonwealth fosters? This book is a must read for scholars and researchers of British politics and British history.

The Commonwealth and Britain

Dennis Austin

Routledge
Taylor & Francis Group
REVIVALS

First published in 1988
by Routledge & Kegan Paul Ltd.

This edition first published in 2024 by Routledge
4 Park Square, Milton Park, Abingdon, Oxon, OX14 4RN

and by Routledge
605 Third Avenue, New York, NY 10017

Routledge is an imprint of the Taylor & Francis Group, an informa business

© Royal Institute of International Affairs 1988

Publisher's Note
The publisher has gone to great lengths to ensure the quality of this reprint but points out that some imperfections in the original copies may be apparent.

Disclaimer
The publisher has made every effort to trace copyright holders and welcomes correspondence from those they have been unable to contact.

A Library of Congress record exists under ISBN: 0710213670

ISBN: 978-1-032-57623-7 (hbk)
ISBN: 978-1-003-44028-4 (ebk)
ISBN: 978-1-032-57625-1 (pbk)

Book DOI 10.4324/9781003440284

CHATHAM HOUSE PAPERS · 41

THE

COMMONWEALTH

AND BRITAIN

Dennis Austin

The Royal Institute of International Affairs

Routledge & Kegan Paul
London, New York and Andover

First published 1988
by Routledge & Kegan Paul Ltd
11 New Fetter Lane, London EC4P 4EE
29 West 35th Street, New York, NY 10001, USA, and
North Way, Andover, Hants SP10 5BE

Reproduced from copy supplied by
Stephen Austin and Sons Ltd and
printed in Great Britain by
Redwood Burn Limited,
Trowbridge, Wiltshire.

Library of Congress Cataloging-in-Publication Data

Austin, Dennis, 1922-
    The Commonwealth and Britain.

    (Chatham House papers ; 39)
    Includes bibliographical references.
    1.   Commonwealth of Nations – Foreign relations –
        Great Britain
    2.   Great Britain – Foreign relations –
        Commonwealth of Nations.
I. Title.
II. Series: Chatham House papers ; no. 39.
DA18.2.G7A97   1987   327.41017'1241   87-26324

ISBN 0-7102-1367-0 (Routledge & Kegan Paul)   26324

CONTENTS

For Rani and Anirudha

Tadpole and Taper were great friends. Neither of them ever despaired of the Commonwealth.

(Benjamin Disraeli, *Coningsby*, Bk 1, Ch. 1.)

When philosophy paints its grey in grey, then has a shape of life grown old ... It cannot be rejuvenated but only understood. The owl of Minerva spreads its wings with the falling of the dusk.

(G.W.F. Hegel, *Philosophy of Right*, Preface, 1820)

ACKNOWLEDGMENTS

I owe a great deal to colleagues who, during the writing of this brief essay, schooled me in preparation and substance. Chief among them were Pauline Wickham and Roderic Lyne of the Royal Institute of International Affairs, Peter Lyon of the Institute of Commonwealth Studies, Peter Marshall of the Commonwealth Secretariat, and Keith Panter-Brick, formerly of the London School of Economics.

I am also grateful to Chatham House and to the Lothian Fund for sponsorship and financial support. William Wallace, Director of Studies, brought together a study group at the Institute, which offered advice and criticism on earlier drafts. They too helped to guide me.

Macclesfield, November 1987   D.A.

FOREWORD

When I first considered writing about the Commonwealth 'every drop of ink in my pen ran cold'. There has always been a danger awaiting those who comment on its problems; it is as fiercely defended by those who uphold its fortunes as it is attacked by those who mock its claims. I am more inclined to be numbered among the believers than the sceptics. Even so, I have no wish to suffer the fate of Uzzah who, seeing that the Ark of the Covenant was in danger of falling, sprang forward to steady it, only to be struck dead by Jehovah for his pains.[1]

It seemed prudent, therefore, not to be too active in defence of the modern Commonwealth when starting this essay. I also wondered whether Britain had not come to resemble the Sorcerer's Apprentice, who summoned to his aid forces greater than he could control. Almost fifty states! That was an enormous change from the Commonwealth of the old Dominions whose soldiers had fought alongside the armed forces of the United Kingdom in two world wars. By what process had Britain transformed the Commonwealth into an international association numbering more than a third of the membership of the United Nations? Had it been by design or chance? Had Britain been intelligently devious in seeking to continue the Empire by different means – by what used to be called neo-colonialism – or had the Commonwealth grown without much foresight or intention? And if the latter, as one might suspect of British policy, what common interests are there today to sustain a multiple relationship so haphazardly established?

As I turned these questions over in my mind, I thought it sensible to sketch an outline of the Commonwealth in 1987 by looking at its character in the light of its upbringing before trying to examine the ties of association. In this way the three main sections of the essay took shape – Observations, Metamorphosis and British Interests. Running through each section are the twin themes of design and chance. Did Britain know what it was doing when it encouraged the admission of so many new members, or were successive governments carried along by the force of events which, if not outside their control, were beyond their understanding?

There is in fact little evidence that Britain foresaw, or even reflected upon, the difficulties that enlargement might bring. Both Labour and Conservative governments stumbled along a path of reform:

> It is typically British to imagine that it is possible to reform
> without first being clear about its purpose, without settling the
> value judgements and working out the objectives of the
> reformed institutions. It is assumed that by looking at the
> particular machine, by taking evidence about how the present
> arrangements work, inconsistencies will emerge, obvious
> changes will suggest themselves and the problem will be solved.[2]

Exactly. But the picture is common enough in most societies. In any period of fundamental change there is a familiar paradox. Events seem to move inexorably along a certain path to what becomes, in retrospect, an inevitable end. Meanwhile, policy during these years shifts uncertainly about and tries to find a way forward out of particular problems without any distant prospect in view.

The paradox is part of the stock-in-trade of historians, and I was made aware of the puzzle during a meeting of scholars in the Villa Serbelloni at Bellagio who met to discuss problems arising from conflicting assessments of the end of empire.[3] 'The owl of Minerva spreads her wings with the coming of dusk.' Yes, and the time seemed ripe for study now that the European empires were almost gone. No longer dazzled by the glare of empire, the historians studied the ground beneath their outstretched wings, and it was in the falling dusk of a mild autumn evening that those who met together at the Rockefeller villa tried to describe the time when Britain, France and Belgium had surrendered their authority. In essence, historians are like the aerial photographers of my air force days. They bring back their distant views, neatly framed for approval, or unwind the film of their observations for scrutiny. So it was in Bellagio, in the shade of the tall dark cypresses which mark out the terraced steps down to the sunshine of the lake. The pictures presented for examination showed clearly the sequence of events which shaped the Commonwealth: India 1947, Ghana 1957, Kenya in the 1960s, Malta and the Caribbean islands, southern and central Africa and the Pacific. There were repeated grants of independence as the balance between Empire and Commonwealth tilted away from British rule.

So much is clear with hindsight. But had we surveyed the world in 1945, the assessment would have been different. We would have looked out over a familiar landscape of dependent territories and sovereign states. An intelligent observer of a mathematical turn of mind might have predicted, by a simple Markov chain of probability, the increase in the number of independent nations over future years, but politicians are not mathematicians. To predict is easy, to face the immediacy of events is quite another matter. Secretaries of state, colonial governors and nationalist politicians had to decide what to do in all the uncertainties of the present. Statistical determination did not enter the vocabulary of action. Nor did politicians willingly accept as inevitable what they were later obliged to endorse. Arguments which purported to show that the independence of South Asia was bound to have effect elsewhere within the empire would have encountered beliefs that 'India was different', 'Ceylon was unusual' or 'Africa is not Asia'.

Only from the vantage point of today, looking back over the post-war years, is the direction clear. The hunt was up and colonialism was its prey, from India in 1947 to Zimbabwe in 1980. But that was not how it appeared at the time. Hugh Tinker might write: 'August 1947 demonstrated that British governments of whatever political complexion could dispose of the remaining imperial possessions as soon as they wished. The politicians were not slow to dismantle the imperial museum.'[4] But that was too indulgent. Historians can indeed lay bare what was not seen at the time. They are, after all, grander than mere pilots. They are like gods who ride above the chronology of events, but they falsify their trade if they translate the consequences of a particular set of events back into the intentions of those who acted at the time. In brief, it was far from clear that the

European empires were doomed. In 1947 the French were success-
fully quelling an armed uprising in Madagascar. Settlers were
moving out again to Kenya and Rhodesia. Between 1945 and 1955
recruitment into the colonial service increased by more than 50 per
cent, and colonial rule was reimposed in Southeast Asia. Academics
were beginning to map the retreat of British rule via 'representative'
and 'responsible government', but no one was prepared to put a
timetable to it, or to assert that Commonwealth membership would
follow independence. Reforms were carried out in many colonies,
but many of these were seen as enabling colonial rule to be more
effective, not as hastening its demise. It was frequently proposed that
this or that colonial administration would move in the direction of
'more participation by the people in the work of government as a
real necessity for lasting social achievement', but that too simply
reflected the way in which the British controlled their colonial
dependants, preferring acquiescence to coercion.[5] Preoccupations in
the Colonial Office in the late 1940s and early 1950s were not with
questions of self-government but with reform of 'native administration' and increases in primary production – margarine from ground-
nuts in Tanganyika, and eggs from the Gambia for the British
breakfast table. The empire which had been harnessed for war was
now needed to establish peace.

Yet by 1980 it was all over, though with an ugly twist of events to
come in the South Atlantic. The empire has gone, and a Commonwealth of almost fifty states stands in its place, although
interpretation is still disputed. Was there always the promise of
emancipation – a bestowal of liberty? Or was it merely the fact of
revolt – a failure of empire? Historians who once charted the
fortunes of the Dominions gave the Commonwealth high praise and
enlisted grand theory in its behalf. They maintained that Edmund
Burke's argument for reconciliation with America – 'I am not
determining a point of law. I am restoring tranquillity' – had now
succeeded. The Commonwealth justified the Empire and was its
final realization. 'It is nothing else than the "nature" of the British
Empire defined, in Aristotelian fashion, by its end.'[6] India was added
to the achievement. 'From 1917 onwards India was accepted in the
conference circle as the "juniormost traveller on the highroad to self-
government" – the same road which the Dominions had already
travelled.'[7]

How splendid such phrases were, and how comforting! One could see how the transformation of Empire into Commonwealth occurred. A pattern of reform was established, which was available, known and applied as a remedy whenever a certain crisis arose in a particular colony that required some rearrangement of power. Precedent created principles of reform, and events enforced their adoption at a quickening pace throughout the colonial Empire.

But it is also possible now to detect a weariness during the 1970s with what remained of colonial rule. The sense of achievement faded. The accession to full Commonwealth membership by India had been a grand occasion. Ghana and Malaya were both received with satisfaction, Nigeria with considerable élan. But the swift transfer of power to colonies hitherto held back from independence as being too small, too divided or too strategically important began to have all the appearance of indifference. The reluctance to retain control was not so much the cost of maintaining a residual empire as the disproportionate effort that might be required to 'restore tranquillity', as in the imperialism of the absurd in Anguilla. Ceremonies of independence came to resemble rituals of retreat; the conversion of colonies into sovereign states was hurried through without much thought for the Commonwealth. And, eventually, the British sought their own release. They ran towards the wicket gate of freedom, divesting themselves as they went of almost the last rock and atoll.

The outcome is the present Commonwealth, described in the opening chapter and re-examined in the conclusions of this brief essay. No attempt is made at prophecy: to look into the future is no less difficult today than it was in 1945. If there is a claim, it is to offer the reader an account which lies somewhere between history and reportage, remembering R.G. Collingwood's warning: 'Contemporary history embarrasses a writer not only because he knows too much, but also because what he knows is too undigested, too unconnected, too atomic. It is only after close and prolonged reflection that we begin to see why things happened as they did, and to write history instead of newspapers.'[8]

1
OBSERVATIONS

The observations described in this opening section are offered as a framework of reference and should be read as a preliminary set of *dicta*. Together they portray an international association of some fifty states which were once colonial dependencies under British rule. Shaped by its origins, the Commonwealth has been a valiant attempt to give institutional expression to the legacy left by the Empire. In its early years it struggled to meet the dilemma which no British government, after the American revolution, had been able to solve: how to square a belief in parliamentary government at home with the denial of its practice abroad. The simplest answer – federal unity – was ruled out. The closed nature of British society preferred to keep the enormous Empire and its problems at arm's length if only not to disturb the delicate balance at Westminster. The difficulty of accommodating Irish members of parliament in the 1880s was instructive in this respect: there was to be no further representation of overseas territories in the Mother of Parliaments, no *l'Angleterre d'outre-mer* on a French model of incorporation.

The problem found an incomplete solution in the idea of Self-Governing Colonies. Local control through local parliaments became the transferred birthright, one might say, of Canadians, Australians, New Zealanders and (some) South Africans. The Commonwealth then became a means of preserving the Empire, for although national interests pushed these settler colonies in the direction of independence, sentiment held them back from separation. There were all the ties of consanguinity between them. In this way, the combination of Dominion autonomy and allegiance to the Crown produced a formula of association which came more and more to resemble that most English of institutions, the club. Members were committed to the rules of association which they tended to make up as they went along. The name-plate was something new in British history: a 'Commonwealth of nations'.

Thereafter, its growth followed a pattern of imitation. The grant of representative government was an ameliorative principle for settler colonies, but it could not be denied in perpetuity to non-European territories without open endorsement of a racial philosophy repugnant to British precepts. The Indian elite, schooled in British beliefs, demanded for themselves what had been granted to the Dominions. They wanted independence but were also willing to accept the formula of Dominion status and Commonwealth membership. In due course, where India led, the Asian, African, Caribbean and Pacific colonies followed.

That roughly has been the Commonwealth's upbringing. What it is today, in 1987 – a century since the first meeting in London of the prime ministers of Britain and its Self-Governing Colonies in the Golden Jubilee year of Queen Victoria – is examined below.

(1) The large increase in membership during the past 40 years transformed the Dominion Commonwealth into something very different

By 1945 Britain, Canada, Australia, New Zealand and South Africa had come close to being a civil society of shared beliefs and agreed ends. Fortified by war, membership was determined as much by social ties as by agreement between governments. It is worth recalling that, despite a strong sense of Dominion nationalism, Britain and the Commonwealth fought the Second World War together under the Crown – Eire excepted – over a longer period than the United States, Russia, Germany and Japan. In 1945–6, though war-weary, Britain and the Dominions were part of the triumvirate of Allied Powers. In Harold Macmillan's phrase, they seemed 'masters of the world and heirs to the future'.[1]

The door was opened for the colonial Empire by India's accession to full Commonwealth status in 1947. A quickening pace of reform emancipated colony after colony. Their entry into the Commonwealth – dependence at nightfall, sovereignty in the morning –

was remarkable. Apart from isolated exceptions – Burma, Palestine, Sudan, Aden – no other colony forbore to apply, no newly independent government failed to be admitted. But the enormous increase in numbers had a qualitative effect. What was once a 'cabinet of governments' is now an international assembly. That exaggerates the past and slightly demeans the present arrangement of Commonwealth meetings, but the price of enlargement – 8 in 1950, 11 in 1960, 21 by 1965, 30 in 1970 and 49 by 1987 – has been a loss of intimacy. Robert Menzies, an old-guard prime minister, marked the change:

> We now have many more Prime Ministers – the better part of thirty – and the large Conference Room at Marlborough House is jammed full of people. Quiet discussion is impossible. Each speech is one made to something like a public meeting, and political leaders seldom make the helpful concessions which are possible in a small and friendly conference.[2]

The consequence was not all loss. Intimacy had imposed its own restraints. By the 1970s, British governments felt better able to pursue their own interests. The move towards Europe, for example, was never easy, but it would have been much more difficult had there been no loosening and widening of Commonwealth ties. One must also suppose that had India and the African and Caribbean countries not opted to join, South Africa would not have withdrawn in 1961. That would certainly have imposed additional problems on Britain: far better to have apartheid outside than under the Commonwealth net. Enlargement, therefore, brought its own freedoms, not least for the United Kingdom.

(2) The Commonwealth today is weak in symbolism, lacking strong ties of association

The great difference is between Commonwealth and Empire. The latter was rich in imagery, attracting devotion as well as hostility, compelling respect and evoking comparisons with Rome.[3] A Commonwealth of sovereign states cannot compete in these terms. Its history since 1945 has been a moving away from any central purpose or common bond, a centrifugal process that has seen what was once a virtue yield to necessity: the Commonwealth is now praised not for its unity but its variety, and for its diversity rather than its strength.

The Crown is no substitute for this loss of identity. Sentimentalists in Britain like to regard royalty as the supreme icon, and the Queen is certainly Commonwealth-minded. No one doubts the strength of her devotion or the gentle dignity brought to Commonwealth meetings by her commitment. But the Crown is no longer a Commonwealth-wide focus of personal loyalty, and, alongside republican presidents and local monarchies, it cannot be so. The Queen's position as titular Head of the Commonwealth, and actual Head of State for 18 of its members,* does not alter the fact.

One by one the unifying symbols have lapsed – no Imperial Airways, no shared citizenship, no common flag, no joint allegiance, no eagles, no trumpets – and as the symbolism has diminished, so too has the stock of largely British ideas which once infused the politics of its members. Perhaps it is asking too much today to expect that Britain should still attract imitation of its politics, but there was a time when the Dominions took it for granted that they shared a common heritage – Westminster, Whitehall, free elections and the rule of law. The Indian and Sri Lankan elites were caught up in liberal values for many years, including a belief in gradual change, the commitment to constitutionality and a concern for the common good. There is nothing today to parallel that influence, no modern Ruskin, no John Stuart Mill, T.H. Green or Tawney, and no novelist of the Commonwealth remotely equal to the romantic interpreters of Empire: no *Kim*, no *King Solomon's Mines*.[4] Socialists, too, in many Commonwealth Third World countries have ceased to be Fabian-influenced, preferring to look to Havana or Moscow and to centralized modes of control rather than to principles of justice. In 1926 the Balfour Committee on imperial relations talked of 'free institutions' as the 'life blood' of the Commonwealth.[5] In these terms the present association is decidedly anaemic.

(3) The erosion of political freedom has washed away belief in Commonwealth values

Until recently it was possible to see the Commonwealth as a liberal cross-section of the international community. A belief in the supremacy of parliaments rather than parties, a trust in free elections, and an absence of torture and political detention were a

*Seventeen if Fiji becomes established as a republic.

common legacy. Over the past two or three decades such beliefs have been pushed aside. Governments have become fearful in the face of political disorder. Economic failure, international pressures and the spread of communal conflict have soured the politics of a number of Commonwealth members – India, Sri Lanka, Malaysia, Fiji – which were recognizably liberal in the early years of their independence.

Whether the Commonwealth can turn its back on the past and accept the good and the bad without qualification is still an open question, although to tolerate everything and everyone reduces the association to very little. What becomes of the Commonwealth Parliamentary Association, or of numerous declarations issued from Commonwealth conferences on individual rights and racial equality? The puzzle is to know where the search for new mechanisms of control will end. The horrors of Uganda did in fact prove too much even for Commonwealth practice. Idi Amin never attended a Commonwealth conference, and James Callaghan made it clear that the Field Marshal would not be welcome at the London Heads of Government meeting in 1977. African governments, however, including several Commonwealth members, were willing to accept Amin as Chairman of the Organization of African Unity in 1975–6, although Tanzania, Zambia and Botswana, to their credit, boycotted the OAU meeting in Kampala. The controversy at Vancouver over Fiji shows how difficult it is to draw a line between 'acceptable' and 'unacceptable' members.

(4) The Commonwealth has a disproportionate number of small states which need protection from themselves as much as from international predators

The equivalents of the ancient world's city-states have not fared well in the twentieth century. Frenzy is as likely as democracy in the small island states of the Caribbean, Pacific and Indian Oceans. Not only does the burden of the modern world crush the poor and vulnerable; the intimacy of political life excites passion. Smallness can be very disagreeable, particularly when remoteness is added to a lack of resources to take care of the economy and administration. Twenty-seven – over half – of the Commonwealth's states have a population of under one million inhabitants, and eight more contain between one and five million. In 1983, in the aftermath of the Grenada adventure, the Heads of Government met in New Delhi and commissioned a study of the problem. The report which appeared two years later – *Vulnerability: Small States in the Global Society* – is long on description, short on remedy. The problem is not difficult to define, but no one knows what to do about the absurdity of sovereign mice and sovereign elephants consorting together as equals.

(5) The Commonwealth has long ceased to be an economic framework for policy

As in matters of high policy, so in trade and finance. The Commonwealth is now too diffuse, plural and divided, and its members too nationally conscious, for it to be an arena for collective action. The empire of free trade and of Commonwealth preferences is as dead as the empire of colonial possessions. The world which was held in place by British power and wealth has been transformed. New poles of power exert a very different force – the strength of the US economy, the regulations of the General Agreement on Tariffs and Trade, the growth of Japan, the rise of new industrial nations in the Far East and the coming together of Western Europe. These are the lineaments of a world in which Britain struggles to adjust an outworn economy and in which the Commonwealth is unable to play any cohesive role. Commonwealth preferences were finally discarded in the 1970s when tariff advantages were granted by the EEC to the African, Caribbean and Pacific countries affiliated under the Lomé Convention, with the result that Britain now imposes quotas and preferences against several non-associated Commonwealth countries whose exports are said to threaten British/ EEC output.

Overseas aid programmes continue to use agencies such as the Commonwealth Fund for Technical Cooperation (CFTC) as a sensible conduit. But they, too, have been diminished in recent years, not only by the government's preference for bilateral agreements with selected Third World countries (not all of which are Commonwealth members), but by alternative funding through the European Development Fund, to which Britain is obliged to contribute.

Commonwealth governments are well aware that they can do little more than survey such problems. They have no collective strength to tackle them. The reports which appear biennially from the Heads of

Government conferences contain long commentaries on international debt, inflation, poverty, North-South divisions and the transfer of resources. Meanwhile, the world grows more intractable, forcing Britain away from the wider Commonwealth world to the richer, narrower confines of Europe. For the Commonwealth to come into its own as an association of rich and poor, of developed and developing countries, the primary concerns of the major trading nations would have to be recast in terms of the Brandt Report or the more recent study, *Our Common Future*.[6] Current preoccupations among the wealthy are very different: they struggle to preserve their own standard of living. A Britain that oscillates between a Conservatism-of-the-market and Socialism-in-one-country certainly leaves little room for the redirection of energies in favour of a revived colonial past. There is scant enthusiasm either, since many are disposed to blame the habits of Commonwealth and Empire for British sloth.

(6) The Commonwealth functions better at the level of specialized interests than at the level of national governments

Descriptions of the network of voluntary organizations and professional groups show a variety of links between Commonwealth countries. A few are pan-Commonwealth, others are directed towards helping the movement of students, administrators, engineers, doctors, artists and scholars between one Commonwealth country and another. Many try to maintain professional standards among architects, pharmacists, quantity surveyors, veterinary surgeons, etc. Nearly all are based in London. They bear out other observations that the Commonwealth is an association in which people get along better than governments:

> In international and racial policies the frontier between reality and nothingness was approached in the post-war decade in which, paradoxically, the Commonwealth idea acquired content and substance in respect of social, economic and educational cooperation, such as it had not hitherto possessed.[7]

Cooperation at this unofficial level helps a little to give substance to a Commonwealth identity, but it also attracts political interest. There has been a record of interference, as over the Edinburgh

Games in 1986, when athletes were forbidden by their governments to run, walk, jump, bicycle or swim in the belief that Britain needed to be rebuked over South Africa. The explanation for such meddling is simple. However earnestly the Commonwealth of good deeds tries to operate below the level of governments, many of its voluntary bodies are dependent on state funding and are vulnerable to pressure. There is – unfortunately – no 'unofficial Commonwealth' separate and safe from the world of national governments and Heads of Government meetings.

(7) The Secretariat has multiplied its functions without greatly strengthening its position

The Secretariat was established in 1965 'primarily to organize consultations and the exchange of information'. The original proposal for such a body goes back to the Imperial Conference of 1907 but its implementation was delayed for more than half a century by apprehension in London that a secretariat might impede its authority and by suspicion among Dominion leaders that their autonomy might be circumscribed. The first Secretary-General was a Canadian, Arnold Smith, who weathered the crisis over Rhodesia after November 1965. His successor is Shridath Ramphal from Guyana, who subsequently enlarged the office. The Secretariat now has some 400 staff and a budget of £5 million, of which Britain contributes 30 per cent, Canada 17 per cent and Australia 9 per cent. Enlargement, said Shridath Ramphal, was 'a necessary growth, necessary both to dissolve the residual film of Anglo-centricity that was distorting its image and to support its increasingly functional dynamism.'[8]

That was bold, but probably meant little more than restricting (British) Foreign and Commonwealth Office influence, and trying to get something done. The result, however, has been an enlargement of the Secretariat's own difficulties, most notably with London. The main quarrel with Mrs Thatcher's administration came in 1985 over the question of sanctions against South Africa. The wider issue has been whether the Secretariat should marshal the Commonwealth behind collective policies. At the Heads of Government meeting in the Bahamas in October 1985, and in London in August 1986, the Secretariat sought to put its weight behind a policy of sanctions. The reasoning was simple: sanctions had helped to bring Rhodesians to the conference table in 1980, and should now be employed on a Commonwealth-wide basis to compel white South Africans to change their skin.

But Shridath Ramphal was rebuked: 'It was never envisaged that the Commonwealth would be or become an instrument for joint executive action.'[9] Lord Home, a former prime minister and Secretary of State for Commonwealth Relations, voiced his own concern in a letter to *The Times* on 8 July 1986: 'The Government should resist any attempt to turn the Commonwealth into an executive instrument of policy.'

In this way the reversal of roles was complete. It is London now which resists any attempt to enforce 'Commonwealth policies', notably of course on Britain, and one may reasonably conclude that the days of collective action by Commonwealth governments is as dead as the years of British dominance.

Perhaps one should add here a subordinate observation, namely, that *the view of Britain as isolated within the Commonwealth because of South Africa needs qualification.*

There was criticism at the 1985 Nassau conference of the tone of Mrs Thatcher's objections to sanctions. There were also strong declarations of principle. But moral attitudes are rarely the basis of policy. There are also interests. To be in favour of (British) sanctions was worth a nod of approval by Commonwealth leaders, if only for their domestic audiences; but to suppose that they were all so committed to ending apartheid as to prefer the disruption of Commonwealth ties with Britain to compromise over policy towards South Africa miscalculates the variety of their interests.

By 1987 Commonwealth governments had begun to draw back from confrontation over South Africa. Some are remote from the problem. Others are too closely involved to be able to act. Zimbabwe and Zambia would like to call down fire from heaven onto Pretoria, but they too are afraid of being burned and have hesitated to implement the full package of sanctions drawn up at Nassau. Nor is it clear how threats or decisions to leave the Commonwealth would help the problem. Britain is a key actor, since southern Africa is one area where it still has not only interests but some influence. Better, therefore, to argue with London than to ostracize its government. And, to do that, Commonwealth ties need to be retained.

South Africa, one might say, has helped to rescue the Commonwealth from boredom but at the cost of rather too much excitement. And no doubt it would be prudent to enter a *caveat*. Interests do not always triumph over emotion. One cannot rule out a heightened sense of frustration in Lusaka, Harare or Lagos, particularly if it chimes with local advantage. The sight of apartheid at bay – defiant and repugnant – does not make compromise easy, and the moral gesture of withdrawal from Commonwealth membership may still have an appeal.

(8) Conflict among Commonwealth countries is now more frequent than confrontation between Britain and other member governments

Within the past two decades, Pakistan resigned its membership because of recognition for Bangladesh; Tanzania invaded Uganda; Bangladesh and Sri Lanka are ambivalent about their relations with India; Nigeria and Ghana have expelled each other's citizens; the West Indies were divided over Grenada until rescued by the United States; and Fiji has raised the issue of racial conflict in a new setting. The Commonwealth praises itself for being unlike the United Nations. But it should be remembered that, although the UN lacks some of the friendliness of the Commonwealth, it does have the merit of universality which gives it authority, and of institutions – including the Security Council – which can bring force to bear.

Quarrels between member governments ought not to lead to resignations; but because the ethos of association implies an intimacy of relationship, it can work against Commonwealth unity when a particular member is affronted. The Commonwealth does not have the thick skin of the UN, nor perhaps its tradition of hypocrisy, and is all the more vulnerable on that account.

(9) Britain's position is not coequal but distinct

The list is long that creates the distinction – the presence of the Queen, the location of the Secretariat, the number of voluntary organizations, the City and its capital markets, the trading position of the United Kingdom and its membership of the EEC, plus its history as 'original member'. Until recently, most of the crises which disturbed the Commonwealth also arose from British policy: the attack on Suez, negotiations for entry into Europe, legislation on citizenship and immigration, and policies towards Rhodesia and South Africa. Each became a measure of the extent to which others saw membership as determined by their association with Britain. But that may be changing.

Despite a falling off of public interest and the government's coolness towards the Secretariat, one suspects Britain is more concerned about the Commonwealth and its future than are other member countries. It is easier to rid oneself of the burden of empire than to escape its legacies. Britain is rooted in its colonial past, a condition that produces both opportunities and obligations. There are sentimental attachments and possibilities of influence. The diminution of world standing is compensated a little by new ties through Commonwealth membership, and it is by no means clear that any British government would want to see them abrogated. (Would any prime minister, even today, view with indifference a large number of resignations from the Commonwealth, whether as the result of British policy or from some other cause?) Commonwealth, therefore, becomes the consolation prize for loss of empire, although the reality is that post-colonial relations are characteristically double-edged. On the one hand, they draw on a reservoir of understanding which may help towards international stability, enhancing Britain's standing in the world; on the other hand, they are a prey to suspicion and to exaggerated expectations.

The Commonwealth is also an evocation, a memory of a different past, extending over more than four centuries of empire when the sea was a means to fortune. Now the maritime story is closed up – no colonies, no merchant fleet, no command of the sea – and Britain is once again a continental power, its troops stationed permanently in Europe. Yet still the Commonwealth evokes the past, sitting 'crowned on the grave of empire' and beckoning.

The most visible legacy of that past are the Asian and West Indian communities who have settled in the United Kingdom. Even if a multiracial Commonwealth does not survive, a multiracial population in Britain will remain a permanent feature of city life. Whether the presence of non-white minorities in Britain strengthens or weakens Commonwealth ties is also open to debate, but the debate itself helps to reinforce the importance of Britain at the centre of Commonwealth interests.

* * *

Most empires bequeath legacies of religion, law, frontiers, language, dress and social custom. The unusual feature of Britain's relations with its former colonies has been the search for a way of continued association. The happy chance of the title 'Commonwealth' – a description well established in English history, transferred to Massachusetts in the seventeenth century and later to Australia – enabled the advantages of a multinational society to be contained within formal structures under the Crown. The contrast is with the struggle by France to establish a post-colonial relationship on the basis of language, a catchment wider of course than the former French empire. The Commonwealth, however, exists very formally. There is a list of members, a subscription, a secretariat, a Commonwealth Foundation, and a biennial meeting of Heads of State: the club is an active association.

The Commonwealth owes its cohesion to history. What else binds its members together? They are not an alliance for specific ends, or a regional body for local needs; there is, today, no great directive force or animating principle. At worst, the Commonwealth is rancorous, more like than unlike the UN. But at its best it is a sensible, non-shrill network of cordial relationships extending from the meetings of prime ministers and presidents to training programmes and exchanges between individuals. Its primary role at the highest level is educative. Its principal virtue is, or ought to be, a wish to understand. Its enticement for Britain is the sense of international importance that it engenders.

What is not clear, though the evidence is encouraging, is whether the Commonwealth has acquired endurance. It has in fact survived numerous points of crisis which were thought at the time to be fatal, and it has persisted over a longer period of time than is commonly recognized. India's membership is of forty years standing, that of Canada, Australia and New Zealand over twice that span, plus their nineteenth-century history as Self-Governing Colonies. Against this background the Commonwealth is beginning to acquire almost the status of a Grade I listed building: its demolition may not be allowed, although whether, like other historic structures, it will come to house more than the relics of its past is another matter. For the present, it exists, and Heads of Government have been willing to attend its meetings. The Commonwealth has also proved adaptable, both in redefining the position of the Crown so that republics might be established, and in accommodating a large measure of open disagreement. Although at the margins of national interest, its fragmentation would signify the failure of the international world to sustain a friendly mode of association. In short, its member governments have shown a readiness to trust the past as a basis for the future.   Mr H. Hatterr would have approved:

> 'I found quite lately', says a former Governor of Bombay Presidency, 'a traditionary order at Government House Dapoorie, near Poona, which directed the sentry on guard to present arms if a cat or dog, jackal or goat, entered or left the house during certain hours of the night because it was the ghost of the former Governor, who is still remembered as one of the best and kindest of Englishmen'.[10]

2

METAMORPHOSIS

At the widest reaches of optimism, when the Commonwealth was seen not only as important but permanent, it was argued that the relationship between Britain and the Dominions should be viewed teleologically. In its beginning was its end – a reconciliation of empire and liberty or, more classically expressed, *imperium* and *libertas*.[1] No one today, looking at the Commonwealth and the changes that have taken place within it since the 1960s, could sustain a comparable vision. All too often in the 'new Commonwealth' there has been the fallacy of hope and the erosion of liberty. Better, therefore, to see the association simply as a linear movement through different stages of growth and decline. The following sections trace these changes from the early years after the Second World War to the present position. The record is useful as an amplification of the observations described earlier and as a basis for the analysis of policy which occupies the final chapter.

In broad terms, three phases can be marked out – brightness, diminished light and dusk. They are not sharply delimited, but the mood they convey corresponds with the sequence of events and changes of perception over the past forty years. They are described from the standpoint of London, but it would not be difficult to find corroborative evidence in other Commonwealth capitals.

a. HIGH NOON

Even if the high noon of the post-war Commonwealth were a false light – bright images on a screen – the phrase is apt, since illusion

19

was important to the leaders. Perhaps, too, the Commonwealth has always belonged more to the empire of the mind than to the world of fact, and it is not difficult to show that it did indeed shine forth not merely as the after-glow of empire but in its own bright image.

In 1943 Harold Macmillan watched the Allied armies parade in victory through Tunis, and the words he used, briefly quoted earlier, are worth amplifying:

> My mind went back to Kitchener's army and the battle of the Somme. I had always thought that they were the finest formations that had ever taken the field. But now I had to admit that the First and Eighth Armies were just as good. These men seemed on that day masters of the world and heirs of the future.[2]

Imagination and power were the twin themes of these early years, not always fused together but held in unison for a time. Because the Commonwealth and Empire had helped to sustain Britain's commitment to victory, they were naturally seen as adjuncts to British power. It was as if Sir John Seeley had been right as long ago as 1883 when he had warned that, if England did not lift itself up by means of its empire to the level of the United States and Russia, it would 'sink to the level of a purely European power, looking back as Spain does now to the great days when she was a world state'.[3] Old arguments were employed, often in extravagant vein, as in the 1949 pamphlet *Imperial Policy*: 'It is sometimes forgotten', said the Conservative and Unionist Office, 'that the potential strength of the British Empire and Commonwealth is greater than that of either the United States of America or the USSR' – an assertion that was to be repeated in later years, in respect not of the Commonwealth but of Western Europe.

Despite the drabness of the immediate post-war years, the belief persisted that Britain was the centre of an interlocking group of nations as distinct from its ally the United States as from its opponents the communist powers. The familiar image of the three interlinked circles of Europe, the United States and the Commonwealth was evoked, and any suggestion that Britain might become a primarily European power was sharply rejected. Clement Attlee informed the House of Commons in May 1948, after the signing of the (European) Brussels Treaty, that he was disturbed by the suggestion ... that we might somehow get closer to Europe than to our Commonwealth. The Commonwealth nations are our closest friends. While I want to get as close as we can with the other nations, we have to bear in mind that we are not solely a European Power but a member of a great Commonwealth and Empire.[4]

And, in more expressive language, Winston Churchill:

We are bound to further every honest and practical step which the nations of Europe may take to reduce the barriers which divide them. But we have our own dream and our own task. We are with Europe but not of it. We are linked but not comprised. We are interested and associated but not absorbed, and should European statesmen address us in words which were used of old: 'Shall I speak for thee to the King or the Captain of the host?', we shall reply with the Shummanite woman, 'Nay, Sir, for we dwell among our own'.[5]

If any unkind observer were disposed to add up the wealth and soldiers of the great powers, it was still possible to point to the non-material advantages of an association of free nations. Was 'even Great Britain without the support of the Commonwealth a great power in the sense in which the term has come to be accepted today?'. The answer, wrote Professor Mansergh in 1948, replying to his own question, was 'clearly in the negative'. But he went on to assert (and the argument is very much of its time): 'The lesson of 1940 is surely that the acceptance of material resources as the final criterion of power is no reliable guide.' Although there had been 'a redistribution of power' within the Commonwealth, there was 'no reason to assume that the strength of the whole has been thereby diminished'.[6]

The Commonwealth was only gradually altered in character. The sands of Empire began to run out – most, but not all – into the hourglass of the Commonwealth.[7] Independence in south Asia exacted its price in the brutality of partition, but the decision by India, Pakistan and Ceylon – a Hindu state, an Islamic republic and an ancient Buddhist society – to remain associated with Britain reassured rather than disturbed those who were Commonwealth believers. Admittedly, some of the pronouncements by Nehru ran counter to assumptions in London. They foreshadowed a loosening of Commonwealth ties, the start of the long quarrel over South Africa, and a distancing of the 'new Commonwealth' from the old; but the first of the neutrals had not yet moved all the way to non-alignment. In popular discourse, India was 'more west than east', as during the Korean war. Pakistan was a member of the South-East Asian Treaty Organization; Ceylon had concluded a defence treaty with Britain. And the United Kingdom was still a major power, a nuclear power, in control of a sea-linked chain of imperial defence across the world: Gibraltar, Malta, Egypt, Cyprus, Aden, Singapore, Hong Kong. It was skilfully engaged in the 1950s in putting down a communist insurrection in Malaya; it had troops not only east and south of Suez but on the Canal itself. And its training programmes at Sandhurst, Latimer, Aldershot, Belgrave Square and Greenwich were familiar to army, navy and air force officers throughout the Commonwealth. Admittedly, Australia and New Zealand had taken out additional insurance in 1951 with the United States, but that too was seen as complementary to a network of alliances in the free world.

It is true that the British economy was limping along during these years. The prosperity of the 1960s was some way off; but anxiety over sterling and the balance of payments added its own quota to the belief that the Commonwealth could be used as a springboard for expansion. The aim expressed at the Montreal conference in 1948 was 'an expanding Commonwealth in an expanding world'. Ground-nuts in East Africa, eggs in The Gambia, a Colonial Development Corporation and an Overseas Food Corporation were part of a programme of colonial development unmatched in pre-war years. (If there was disappointment later in East Africa over ground-nuts, it was offset by success in Asia under the Colombo plan.) These hopes were conceived in familiar surroundings. The sterling area (minus Canada) was still responsible for financing a quarter of the world's trade: not until 1954 was sterling convertible into non-dollar currencies, not until 1958 was it possible to convert into dollars, and more than half the United Kingdom's exports went to Commonwealth markets. In addition, Britain was still the largest customer and supplier for all Commonwealth countries except for Canada. Economic worries continued, but since these concerned sterling and dollar shortages, the remedies were also looked for within a Commonwealth/North American framework.

22

Nor was imagination lacking. The vision of an expanding Commonwealth took in more than the material benefits of membership. In March 1949 Dr Evatt, Australian Foreign Minister, listed the virtues of this 'unique group', the first being that it was 'quite impossible to treat the British Commonwealth of Nations as based on mere community of interest, or mere purposes of common defence and the like'. There was 'kinship, kingship and practical comradeship'.[8] The inclusion of the Asian members not only extended 'the bounds of democratic freedom which reflects the spirit and steadfast purpose of the Commonwealth, but gave a balance and breadth to all our deliberations'. Nehru, always interested in the morality of things, was quick to respond. He was not, he said, 'used to the ways of the market place'. He thought it 'better to keep a cooperative association going which may do good in this world rather than break it [and] the fact that we have begun this new type of association with a touch of healing will be good for us, good for them, and I think good for the world'.[9] Such sentiments persisted for a long time.[10] They were expressed in flattering terms by Peter Frazer, Prime Minister of New Zealand, who declared that 'independence within the Commonwealth was independence plus'.

Behind the vision lay the assumption of shared values within a shared political culture. It was as if Macaulay's belief in the superiority of European civilization had been justified, 'that by good government we may educate our subjects into a capacity for better government [until] having become instructed in European knowledge they may, in some future age, demand European institutions'. In more modest vein, Commonwealth leaders recalled the phrases of the Balfour Committee: 'free institutions' – shared ground for a political belief which made sense of the second phrase in the *Report*: 'free cooperation is its instrument'. It was particularly gratifying to the United Kingdom at the centre of this historically created group, whose numbers were steadily increasing as nationalist demands were turned into Commonwealth agreements. Where the process might end, no one could say. In the 1950s there were thought to be barriers to independence for the poor, the small and the defenceless, and Dom Mintoff astonished the Conservative government in 1955 by requesting not independence for Malta but 'integration with Britain', a legitimate if unusual end to colonial status.[11]

High noon indeed: but, paradoxically, not without shadows cast by events. The transmutation of empire into Commonwealth was often troubled – Malaya under attack, Mau Mau in Kenya, the employment of troops (briefly) in the Gold Coast in 1948, and in Nigeria the following year. The constitution of Guyana was suspended in 1953, Seretse Khama was exiled from Bechuanaland, the Kabaka exiled from Uganda. The Commonwealth was now a multiracial association which included white South Africa. It was also a 'Commonwealth of nations', among which were several states, of which Pakistan was perhaps the most conspicuous, whose hold on national unity appeared very tenuous.

For the present, however, all was well, or was thought to be well. The Labour Party, traditionally anti-imperialist, now looked with an almost proprietorial pride upon the new Commonwealth as part of a world with which a post-imperial Britain could consort comfortably. Similarly, there were elements within the Conservative Party which looked kindly on the British Commonwealth, not only as a segment of the non-American English-speaking world but as representing, in some degree, the continuation of empire by other means. Sentiment and advantage were held together by a linked imagination. Within each member country there were still elements of political and administrative practice derived from a shared past. Commonwealth prime ministers were close to Britain in outlook either as wartime colleagues or as representatives of the first generation of nationalist leaders: Mackenzie King, St Laurent, Menzies, Frazer, Nehru, the two Senanayakes, Liaqat Ali Khan, Nazimuddin. The least known, and perhaps the least 'British', was D.F. Malan, an ominous change from Smuts. The Commonwealth was thus an established part of a world order, and belief in the advantages of membership rested on these shared ideals. A cautious observer might have questioned what would happen if the advantages diminished or the ideals became tarnished. Would the vision fade if the power were not there to sustain it? But such doubts would have been brushed aside. So much was dark in this post-war decade, whereas the Commonwealth was a bright area of hope.

b. AFTERNOON LIGHT

Menzies' *Autobiography*, under this title, reflects a period of uncertainty. The shadows lengthen, the questions multiply. Should there be a two-tiered Commonwealth of fully sovereign and locally autonomous members? What purpose was served by so diverse a membership? Perhaps it was true that the 'new Commonwealth' was no more than a transitory association, surviving only long enough to enable Britain to move gracefully away from an empire it could no longer sustain? The 1939 Commonwealth had not been like that, but the transfer of power to new members was gathering pace at an astonishing rate. Moreover, other empires were dissolving: Holland, France, Belgium, even Spain in a halting kind of way. It was no longer possible to see the United Kingdom as a unique 'imperial power turned Commonwealth', and the argument began to be used that Britain had simply been a prescient forerunner of a wider European movement away from empire. That was to ignore the history of Dominion self-government, but it was certainly true that other post-imperial relationships were being forged, not only between France and *la francophonie* but in the association of a number of Third World ex-colonies with the EEC. The Commonwealth was unusual in the variety and antiquity of many of its members, but its significance began to be blurred by the flurry of decolonization which filled the United Nations with the newly independent.

There were other worrying developments. The concept of 'superpower' divided the world, notably during the Cuban crisis in 1962. Under Harold Wilson's premiership in 1964–70 and 1974–6, the United Kingdom still insisted on its 'world role'. Willing to defend Malaysia against its neighbours, ready to intervene and suppress army mutinies in Kenya, Tanganyika and Uganda, it continued to protect what were seen as Commonwealth interests overseas. But the limits to British power were already evident, and throughout these middle years of anxiety there was a growing preoccupation with Europe. It seemed that NATO membership and troops stationed permanently on the mainland were not enough: new associations of great economic power were being formed from which Britain was excluded. At the end of the 1950s the Conservative government had tried to assemble a counterbalancing group in the shape of a European Free Trade Area,* but in August 1961 the first application to join the EEC opened a debate on the advantages of Commonwealth and Europe.

And still the transformation of empire into Commonwealth went on. In the early 1960s the population of the remaining colonies and protectorates was down to 35 million scattered over some forty

*Britain, Denmark, Norway, Sweden, Switzerland, Portugal, Austria and Iceland.

territories. The speed with which decolonization now began to be carried out by a Conservative government was astonishing. Her Majesty's Government, Iain McLeod was reported as saying, had no intention of being the last colonial power in Africa alongside the Portuguese, although in fact that was eventually to be the case in southern Africa. Both McLeod and Macmillan were carried swiftly along before the winds of change, and huffed and puffed a little on their own account to make them blow. The 1962 Commonwealth conference welcomed as new members Trinidad and Tobago, Sierra Leone and Tanganyika, agreed to the future membership of Uganda and Kenya, and took note of the addition of Singapore, Borneo and Sarawak to Malaya to form a Federation of Malaysia. The Commonwealth was growing in proportion as the Empire was shrinking: loss was balanced by gain and there were few defaulters.[12]

The conversion took place in such a way as to enable nationalist leaders to see membership as a natural accompaniment to independence. Yet there was a difference from the early years, a lack of caution, almost a recklessness in the way in which colonies were pushed into freedom. Independence was granted wherever it could be presented as legitimate. The Central African Federation was broken up in 1963: Zambia and Malawi became independent, and when a flag of revolt went up in Salisbury in November 1965, Wilson quickly ruled out military action to bring the colony back under British control. With the exception of Rhodesia, no barrier to independence – neither poverty nor size nor isolation – was allowed to remain. A 'Third World' was being born for which the Commonwealth might begin to see itself not merely as midwife but nurse – except that the world of the rich was getting richer and the poor were condemned to poverty. Britain now lagged behind the prosperous. No longer could it see itself, or be seen, as the centre of a major trading empire, and it was quite unable to provide the aid and investment demanded by its former dependants.

With this sense of diminished importance came a clouding of vision. Following the Anglo-French-Israeli attack on Egypt, there were sour comments in London about Delhi and in Delhi about Britain,[13] offset by protestations of friendship during India's brief war in 1962 with China. 'Free institutions' were now under attack – by military rule in Pakistan, preventive detention in Ghana and tribal conflicts in Nigeria. There was also a new emphasis on regional affiliations. The first conference of independent African states took place in Accra in April 1958, and for a brief period (1958–62) Ghana was merged with two non-Commonwealth countries, Guinea and Mali, in what purported to be a Union of African States. One can understand, therefore, why the view from London was uncertain. The interlocked circles of Europe, the United States and the Commonwealth were out of proportion. The United States was growing in power and wealth. The Commonwealth was amorphous, lacking not only shape but purpose. Harold Macmillan was obliged to enlist the US administration's help over the replacement for Britain's ageing nuclear deterrent, first with Skybolt, then with Polaris. India, too, was looking to Moscow for help with weapons and diplomatic support. The geopolitical map of the world was changing. New regional groupings and new 'superpowers' were forming. What room was there for a non-regional, non-military association which lacked the mechanics of a common market or customs union?

In 1961 South Africa withdrew its membership. The decision might seem to be constructive, at least to the multiracial character of the Commonwealth, but there were disturbing aspects to the break. Was it truly in accord with Commonwealth principles for a member country to be subject to such close scrutiny? Nehru had not liked the possibility in 1949.[14] And, after all, what difference did South Africa's withdrawal make? Critical observers soon noticed that it brought very little change in British/South African relations. Preferential trading arrangements were retained, emigration from Britain continued, investment increased and the Simonstown naval base was still used. As over EEC membership, so over South Africa: neither Labour nor Conservative administrations were willing to allow Commonwealth membership to affect, to any substantial measure, national interests. And what was true for Britain was also the case, it was argued, for others:

Which Commonwealth country would put its relationship with the United Kingdom as its first exclusive interest in world affairs? I am afraid that the answer is, practically none. Would Canada put it above North American solidarity? Would India put it above its desire to lead the uncommitted world? Would Ghana put it above its views of pan-Africanism?[15]

Difficult questions, too, arose over the relationship between peoples. Many early conferences had discussed migration, which was seen as helping the movement of English-speaking people between Britain and the Dominions. Now it was believed that there was need for legislation to define different categories of 'Commonwealth citizen'. There was much uneasiness over what was intended. The Labour government had reassured its critics in respect of the 1948 Nationality Act that 'the metropolitan tradition of hospitality would not be disturbed'. But subsequent legislation falsified the hope: 'Even as the legislators were coming to these comforting conclusions the *Empire Windrush* – the *Mayflower* of the West Indian migration – had sailed from Kingston, and the post-war migration had begun.'[16]

The distinction was sharp. Whereas migration had been a unifying bond, immigration was a disturbing factor. There was more than an element of justice in the change in direction. The imperial government had moved people around the globe: Indians to Fiji, Mauritius, Sri Lanka, Guyana, East Africa and Natal; Chinese to Singapore and Malaya; and West Africans (under slavery) to the Caribbean. Now the point of convergence was Britain itself: West Indians arrived in the 1950s, Indians and Pakistanis in the 1960s. The first race riots in Britain occurred in Notting Hill in 1958. And not only in Britain. There was tension between Malays and Chinese, Indians and Fijians, Tamils and Sinhalese, Africans and Asians, Turks and Greeks. The several member states of a 'Commonwealth of nations' were incapable of incorporating all the citizens of their own nation.

It would be wrong to make the register of these years too exact. It was a time of 'fading light', not dusk; of doubt and uncertainty, a mood – in Britain particularly – of public confidence and private doubts. Duncan Sandys could still say: 'I hope my European friends will not misunderstand me if I say that if I were forced to make this cruel choice [between the Commonwealth and the EEC] I would unquestionably choose the Commonwealth.' But he was able to add: 'Happily we are not confronted with the dilemma.'[17] Hugh Gaitskell for the Labour Party was more robust. In May 1962 he argued that if Britain were to enter the EEC on poor terms it would mean an end to the Commonwealth – 'a step which I think we would regret all our lives and for which history would not forgive us'.[18] In October he repeated the argument in passionate terms: the economic case for entry was 'at best evenly balanced'; the test was political and might mean the end of an independent Britain and of 'a thousand years of history'.[19]

A thousand years or not, the Empire itself was almost at an end. In July 1962 the Colonial Office put up its shutters, leaving the Commonwealth Relations Office as a separate office still. But the latter, too, was said ambiguously 'to resemble the Foreign Service ... except that its work lies among the nations of the Commonwealth and not foreign nations'. The Commonwealth was being brought up to date by redefinition, a familiar pastime among its defenders. At the opening by the Queen of the new Commonwealth Institute in London in 1962, emphasis was laid on 'peoples' rather than governments: 'It is the thread of personal concern and understanding between individual peoples that weaves the strong fabric of the modern Commonwealth.'[20]

There was still a good deal to support the notion of a 'functioning Commonwealth' in the sense of cooperation below the level of governments. There was a continuous movement of teachers, students, doctors, lawyers, administrators, architects, engineers, cricketers and rugby players, as individuals and groups, encouraged by a wide array of associations – so much so that it was possible to argue that 'such inventive dynamism as the Commonwealth has manifested in recent years has been the cause of the expansion and diversification of such movements'.[21]

The good and the bad were mixed, therefore, in the story of these middle years. The believers pointed to the new shoots of growth that they claimed to see. The doubters saw only a steady erosion of belief. Professor Hedley Bull concluded that 'the British people and successive British governments have steadily lost interest in Britain's historic world and Commonwealth role', and that the alternative was not so much a movement into Europe but a retreat 'into the sentiment of insularity and Little Englandism'.[22] Well, perhaps ... Britain was criticized now on all fronts. Its intention to join the EEC meant that Menzies was worried about defence, New Zealand about butter, the Caribbean about sugar, and the African members about the terms of their own association. Nehru talked about Indian textiles, and Diefenbaker spoke in Ottawa about the need to safeguard Commonwealth interests in general. The unkindest cut, however, also came from across the Atlantic:

Britain has lost an Empire and not yet found a role. The attempt to play a separate role ... based on a special relationship with the United States, a role based on being the head of a Commonwealth which has no political structure or unity or strength ... this role is about to be played out.[23]

Alas, poor England! Even its attempt to move from Commonwealth to Europe was blocked by General de Gaulle's calm assurance that Britain was not yet ready 'to transform herself ... without restriction or reservation so as to prefer the European Community to every other connection'. No wonder, then, that these difficult years were ones of doubt – of, at best, an afternoon light.

c. DUSK

It is now possible, in the late 1980s, to see how the past has shaped the future: decolonization almost at an end, Britain fully part of Europe, disputes leading to war between Commonwealth countries, and Heads of Government conferences more akin to United Nations meetings than to reunions among colleagues. These were the hallmarks of the 1970s and early 1980s, making the Commonwealth what it is today. The surprise, beyond expectation, is that it has continued to meet after so bruising a period.

Decolonization reached its end in 1980 when, after protracted negotiations and a cruel civil war, Rhodesia entered the Commonwealth as the Republic of Zimbabwe. The remaining colonies are now those for which the remedy of independence is unavailable – as in Hong Kong, Gibraltar and the Falkland Islands – or so very small as to inhibit even the most ardent internationalist. Alexander Selkirk might have been monarch of all he surveyed, but predators are eager today to dispute his right to govern. In 1983 the invasion of Grenada by the United States placed a large question mark over the reality of the sovereignty which small island communities have struggled to maintain: it may be that there will be no further applications for independence. The unravelling of empire will then be complete.[24]

'Britain is fully part of Europe.' Legally, that is so, and in 1986 both Houses of Parliament at Westminster passed the Single European Act. One may doubt that a substantial transfer of power is taking place between the twelve EC governments and Brussels, but it is clear that the economics of association within a common market are forcing them to yield something to new institutions – the European Parliament, the Commission, the European Court, the European Monetary System and cognate bodies. The long-term consequences cannot be foreseen, but the effect on British policy is more evident each year. Three circles or one? No British government is prepared to abandon what is left of the special relationship with the United States, reinforced after 1981 by the coincidence of like-minded leaders in Washington and London. Meanwhile, the Commonwealth circle grows slack. Throughout the 1970s the Heads of Government met regularly, and there was a sense of triumph in August 1979 when Mrs Thatcher and President Kaunda danced together in Lusaka in anticipation of Zimbabwe's independence the following year. But thereafter there was little occasion for rejoicing. There seemed to be no power, authority or appetite for joint endeavours.

The slackening of Commonwealth ties should have been foreseen. The analysis was there in the recommendations of the (Duncan) *Report on Overseas Representation*, published as early as 1969. The official recognition of change was seen, too, in the merger of the Commonwealth Relations Office with the Foreign Office.

The Duncan Report stands as a signpost to subsequent events.[25] Among its aims was 'the sustaining of Commonwealth ties in a form appropriate to contemporary requirements' – a chilling phrase, reinforced by division of the world into an 'area of concentration' for British diplomacy, and the 'rest of the world' as an 'outer area'. Andrew Shonfield, a member of the Review Committee, was later to acknowledge that 'the latter phrase was unfortunate'; but the substance of the report remained, and Shonfield's comments were representative of a widely held view. 'What the Report was really doing was to spell out belatedly the logic of the end of empire', an end which had been obscured by the way in which 'initially at any rate political relationships within the Commonwealth seemed to provide a ready substitute for the old relationship of empire'.[26]

Here was reality breaking in on dreams. The nightmare of war, Shonfield observed, was retreating from Europe to the insecure states of the Third World, and Britain was being drawn to the peaceful and prosperous. 'Peace' was a qualifiable term, since Europe was still divided into two ferociously armed camps, but throughout the 1970s there was ample evidence of dissent among Commonwealth members.

31

The hope that the Commonwealth might be a peaceful international order, free of enmity between its associates, had to be abandoned. Civil war in Nigeria saw Tanzania and Zambia give formal recognition to Biafra. When Ian Smith aped the American Declaration of Independence, Tanzania and Ghana broke off diplomatic relations with Britain over Wilson's refusal to sanction force against the rebel regime. Twice India and Pakistan went to war, and in 1977 Tanzania invaded Uganda (not only to get rid of Amin but to reinstate Obote, who was then deposed again by a liberation army). Throughout the 1970s – a time when the United States, with Australia and New Zealand in attendance, was committed to war in Southeast Asia – the Commonwealth was divided. If there was distrust of British policy in public speeches by African leaders, there was resentment in Britain over what was said. And when relations deteriorated between Malaysia and Singapore, or between India and Pakistan, the Commonwealth suffered – to the point of Pakistan's withdrawal in 1972.

International relations are necessarily subject to the ebb and flow of power, and the quick turnover of African regimes during these years added to the sense of impermanence. But it was beginning to be clear that the Commonwealth was not very different from the general world of relations between sovereign states. That, too, was a measure of how much had changed since the early brightness of the post-war years. The 'old close intimacy' had gone and the association was now 'functional and occasional'. Menzies' reaction was indicative of a general mood:

> I think that twenty years ago I might have become more impassioned about this matter, but the Commonwealth has changed a lot since then. Its association has become looser. For most of its members the association is, in a sense, functional and occasional.[27]

The view from Ottawa was not very different:

> Canadians might cheer the idea of a multi-racial Commonwealth and be delighted when the prime minister played an important part in a world forum but despite these happy feelings the Commonwealth connection had slipped in importance. The simple truth of the matter was that the remnants of empire

had ceased to matter very much ... Canada was more American now and the multi-racial Commonwealth was less a part of public consciousness than the old all-White Commonwealth had been.[28]

The words echo the Duncan Report's need to sustain Commonwealth links 'in a form appropriate to contemporary requirements'.

What was left to sustain? In general, a great deal, if only because of a *vis inertiae*, the unresisted movement of history which carries much of the past into the future. Even during these troubled years new institutions were appearing, including the Secretariat, the Foundation and the Fund for Technical Cooperation. 'Institutionalization' is not always a happy process. It can signify the need for shoring up as well as for encouraging growth. But the succession of conferences – Singapore 1971, Ottawa 1973, Kingston 1975, London 1977 (to mark the Queen's Silver Jubilee), Lusaka 1979, Melbourne 1981, New Delhi 1983, Nassau 1985 and Vancouver 1987 – was proof of a willingness to keep the association alive, if not actually endorsing Arnold Smith's assertion that it was now 'an effective multilateral instrument ... to shape the future'. Even allowing for the appetite of politicians for travel and for public recognition, there was a residual belief – one must suppose – in the use to which the Commonwealth might be put.

What was it likely to be? Sifting through the agenda and communiqués of the various meetings, two main areas of concern stand out. One was the economic plight of the newly independent member countries – oil prices accelerating, indebtedness beginning to absorb the revenue from exports, inflation threatening costs, and commodity prices starting to fall. The other focus of interest was race, particularly the treatment of the black majority by the white minority in both Rhodesia and South Africa.

Poverty and race. Commonwealth governments could do little about either, but they lodged their complaints at the door of the United Kingdom, since Britain was doubly involved. As a member of the European Community it was now entrenched behind the tariff barriers of the rich. As the residual colonial power in central Africa, and chief trading/investment partner of South Africa, it was open to accusations not only that it was slow to act on behalf of the African majority in Rhodesia, but that it was actively supporting the apartheid regime in Pretoria. South Africa was helping Ian Smith in Salisbury. Britain was trading with South Africa: *ergo* Britain was insincere in its protestations of wanting to end the rebellion in Rhodesia.

* * *

At this point it may be helpful to look more closely at both 'poverty' and 'race' as discussed at the conferences held in various Commonwealth capitals. Since 1977 such gatherings have also included the 'meeting within the meeting', whereby the Heads of Government move away from the main conference centre to a 'retreat': a solace introduced by Pierre Trudeau at Ottawa.

Economic problems
Trade and finance are always discussed, but particular worries were expressed at the Ottawa 1973, Kingston 1975 and Melbourne 1981 meetings. Britain was now beginning to examine its new position in Europe; and Swaran Singh, who led the Indian delegation at Ottawa, voiced a general hope: 'We would like to make a special plea to the United Kingdom to lend its support to the proposal [on commodity price support] and to take steps within the Community to ensure an expeditious examination and solution to the trading problems of the Commonwealth.'[29] That was asking a great deal, although, as Arnold Smith told the Commonwealth governments, 'A Europe including Britain, and the Commonwealth, are not antithetical but complementary. New opportunities for improved markets, friendships and influence in one part of the world are no reason to abandon trading opportunities, old friends and influence elsewhere.'[30]

That might be so, but Britain now had to abide by the rules of what was already established practice within the Community. Edward Heath's government secured transitional arrangements for New Zealand exports and gave what support it could to the enlarged group of 44 Associated States, many of them Commonwealth members, in Africa, the Caribbean, Asia and the Pacific. But, Commonwealth preferences – already dying – were now pronounced dead. Britain, inside the EEC, was in no position to help the new industrializing nations such as India, Malaysia, Singapore and Hong Kong. Negotiations over entry also proved disappointing in respect of particular commodities. There was the special problem of cane sugar. Yet there was nothing that Britain or Commonwealth producers in Australia, Mauritius and the Caribbean could do to check the rising output of European beet sugar.

There were losers and gainers, therefore, from Britain's entry, and Commonwealth leaders had to accept the fact. The Commonwealth did what it could in its own fashion to bridge the divide by enlarging the Fund for Technical Cooperation which had been established at the Singapore meeting, and that was helpful. It then widened its horizons to see what might be done to transform the 'global economy'. The 1970s were the age of Brandt and of North-South dialogue, and the Commonwealth was not found wanting. When the international world, through the UN, turned to consider the problem of underdevelopment or Third World poverty, Commonwealth governments followed suit.

At Kingston, they commissioned the study which appeared two years later as *Towards a New International Economic Order*. The London meeting in 1977 led to the *Report on the Common Fund*, set up to try and help commodity prices. The Lusaka conference authorized a study from which there emerged *The World Crisis: A Commonwealth Perspective*. Melbourne saw the production of *The North-South Dialogue: Making It Work*. (The conference also, more practically, reversed the downward trend in funding for the CFTC.) The reports were stereotyped in their reflection of current preoccupations. They were perhaps cosmetic, designed to make the world appear less forbidding, but – *pace* Hamlet – paint and powder provide aesthetic camouflage for what might otherwise be disagreeable. At the level of academic research and political inquiry they were – and still are – intelligent, educative studies of problems that will certainly be with the world for a long time to come. What effect they have had is a different matter. The world has grown both wealthier and poorer, a division which all the meetings and reports of the UN and the Commonwealth, and the summits of the rich, have done little to change.

Racial conflict

'Race-consciousness lies at the very root of any post-colonial relationship',[31] and after 1960 'African Commonwealth members adopted a self-conscious, often aggressive racial perspective'.[32] That is one view of the events of the time, but racial conflict was also embedded in the events themselves. Nationalist agitation was gathering force in Rhodesia; unrest was spreading in the black townships of South Africa. Both were of concern to Afro-Asian leaders for whom 'race' meant primarily the mistreatment of blacks by whites, particularly of a black nationalist majority by a European settler minority. The extinction of political liberty by local dictators, or communal tension within their own societies, was accorded second place – if any place at all. In Uganda, Idi Amin was now deep in blood, the bones and skulls of his murdered opponents piled high in deep pits beyond Kampala. The death count far exceeded any accusation that could be brought against South Africa, but the Commonwealth was not to be diverted from UDI in Rhodesia or from apartheid in South Africa.

The record of concern went back a long way. Nehru had raised the question of racial discrimination in South Africa at the UN as early as 1947. South Africa withdrew from the Commonwealth in 1961. A decade later, at the Singapore conference, the issue flared again. Edward Heath, newly elected as Conservative Prime Minister and concerned about the Soviet navy's entry into the Indian Ocean, wanted to renew arms sales to South Africa. The Afro-Asian leaders were affronted, and there was a good deal of bad temper. The dispute was referred to a committee and smothered, whereupon the conference settled for a Declaration of Principles: 'We believe in the liberty of the individual ... representative institutions and guarantees for personal freedom ... We recognize racial prejudice as a dangerous sickness.' (Ironically, it was at Singapore that Obote was told of Amin's seizure of power in Kampala and decided not to return.) The Ottawa and Kingston conferences intervened and economic troubles took precedence, but in 1977 South Africa returned to the agenda. If a New Zealand rugby team went to South Africa, should New Zealand athletes attend the Commonwealth games in Edmonton in Canada? On such niceties was based the Gleneagles Agreement, hatched during the prime ministers' 'retreat' from London.[33]

Two years went by and the crisis in Rhodesia came to a head. The guerrilla armies of the Patriotic Front could neither defeat nor be defeated by the Rhodesian army: fighting had spread across the border into Mozambique, and South Africa was being drawn further into the conflict. In Britain, in May 1979, the Conservatives won the general election and brought to office a prime minister, Margaret Thatcher, who carried little of the old Tory sense of empire and nothing of the Fabian belief in Commonwealth, and the Lusaka conference met later that year under the apprehension that racial conflict would divide not only southern Africa but the Commonwealth.

The actual outcome was startling. Against the odds – or because the odds were stacked evenly against both sides – agreement was reached on a packet of reforms, among which were fresh elections, Commonwealth observers and a constitutional conference. In May 1980, following the conference at Lancaster House between all the main contestants – Robert Mugabe, Joshua Nkomo, Ian Smith, Lord Carrington, Bishop Muzorewa, Marxists, Christians, settlers and soldiers – Rhodesia became Zimbabwe, a metamorphosis which evoked admiration from every quarter. The last major British colony entered the Commonwealth as the last member nation.

Again there was an interlude. Peace spread its wings – for a time. And there were other distractions. At Melbourne, it was the inequality between 'North' and 'South'. At New Delhi in 1983, the prime ministers were discomforted, first by the United States' quashing of the murderous rebellion in Grenada a month or so before the conference, then by the declaration of an independent Turkish republic in the northern part of Cyprus a week before they assembled. The delegates could do nothing about either crisis, although an Action Group was established 'to review the position in Cyprus'. The dilemma was familiar. A conference has no power, no troops, no muscle. Policy is reduced to exhortation, and the prime ministers – from their retreat in Goa – issued one more 'Declaration on International Security' and then commissioned the study on the vulnerability of 'smallness'.

The last but one conference examined in this account – Nassau in 1985 – brought the issue of South Africa back to a high pitch of exasperation. The membership now reflected the full maturity of change which had turned the Commonwealth of former Dominions into an international association of sovereign states. The transformation was virtually complete: the change of shape was remarkable. It remained to be seen whether the warmth and clear skies of the Bahamas could lighten the encircling gloom.

d. THE BAHAMAS, 1985
The setting was appropriate. The Caribbean is where the old and new Commonwealth come together. What was once an area of

settler control, plantation labour and Crown rule is now a region of small island-states and mainland territories. They live in the shadow of the United States, which reaches out from time to time either to punish or reward, or to occupy and then withdraw. It is also a region of ideological conflict, Cuba less than an hour's flight from Jamaica to the south, Florida to the north. The Bahamas are the playground for American tourists as well as a staging post for the drug smuggler. The earliest adventurers to the Bahamas were the Spaniards, who enslaved the local Arawak Indians and shipped them to neighbouring plantations. None survived. The British cleared out the Spaniards and pirates, and stayed for 300 years, bequeathing the islands a parliament, a cathedral, some fine botanical gardens and a tourist economy. The capital, Nassau, is a familiar contradiction, its luxury hotels a safe distance from the tenements of the poor, where lines of ragged washing are stretched across dusty streets: the world of the wash-tub versus the tumble-drier.[34]

On the outskirts of the town, the Botanical Gardens offer a novel tourist attraction in the form of a parade of flamingoes who have been taught to march in step. One wonders how the drill was instituted among these handsome birds – elegant in flight, stilt-like on the ground. Meanwhile, a bus-ride away in the playground hotels of Cable Beach, the Heads of Government attending the 1985 conference were also being schooled. However much they might disagree at first, they were expected to march together at the close. The difficulty was that Mrs Thatcher was already out of step over the vexed question of sanctions, for South Africa was again the centre of attraction.

'One subject dominated the politics of the Commonwealth throughout 1985 and the Heads of Government meeting in Nassau – South Africa.'[35] Whereas the New Delhi meeting had merely called for the introduction of 'majority rule on the basis of a free and fair exercise of universal suffrage in a united and non-fragmented South Africa', the Secretariat was now eager to mobilize the Nassau conference. It sketched a possible line of action based on selected sanctions. The purpose was plain: to ratchet up the low level of sanctions already in place – on oil, arms sales and certain types of computer equipment – to a point at which, if they still had no effect, they could be augmented by further measures, monitored by the Secretariat. In this way, the Commonwealth would be moved – step by step, conference by conference, one set of agreements superseded by another – to the goal of mandatory sanctions under international authority.

Thus the conference was put to the test of action. And since apartheid is like sin, no one was for it. Most delegates were also willing to approve a policy of sanctions, since the price demanded was either negligible or even favourable. They divided into four broad groups:

(1) The remote and not directly concerned – Malta, Cyprus, Singapore, the Polynesian and Melanesian islands.

(2) India, Malaysia, West and East Africa, the Caribbean – which were very much concerned but not affected, since they had already cut off trade with South Africa.

(3) The former Dominions – Australia in particular – whose economies, competitive with South Africa's in mining and agriculture, were likely to benefit from sanctions.

(4) The front-line states in central and southern Africa, among which Zimbabwe and Zambia declared their support for sanctions but required protection and compensation, while others, notably Botswana, admitted that they could not in any circumstances bear the cost.

Britain, with its substantial trade and investment in the Republic, was differently placed: it was deeply involved but not directly concerned.

There was deadlock, therefore, in the plenary sessions, and the Commonwealth returned to the querulous times of the 1960s and the 1970s. The United Kingdom was said to be isolated, Mrs Thatcher was under attack. *Britannia contra mundum* is familiar ground for Mrs Thatcher; but others too were keen, as new men, to make their mark – Rajiv Gandhi of India, Brian Mulroney of Canada, Bob Hawke of Australia, Salim Ahmed Salim of Tanzania. The Secretariat was sure that 'the chemistry of the Commonwealth' would work its magic at Nassau as at Lusaka, and so it proved – for a time. While the flamingoes in the gardens tucked their heads beneath their wings, the prime ministers worked hard into the night during their retreat on the smaller resort of Lyford Cay. They returned with an agreement of the kind that, alas, is usually associated with compromise: no one was quite sure what had been settled. But President Kaunda, who had danced with Mrs Thatcher in Lusaka in 1979, announced happily that, like the flamingoes, he and the Prime Minister were back in step.

In one sense, Mrs Thatcher succeeded: 'sanctions' were ruled out and 'measures' substituted, but the prime minister also agreed to prohibit the import of krugerrands into Britain. The Commonwealth too prevailed. A catalogue of further measures was compiled (including the cessation of air links with South Africa) as a warning or 'signal' to Pretoria, which 'some Commonwealth governments' undertook to apply at a later date. It was then agreed that a committee of Eminent Persons should try to visit South Africa to assess the possibilities of dialogue between black and white, and between Pretoria and the outside world – and to report back in six months.

e. MARLBOROUGH HOUSE, 1986

In this way there came about the report of the Commonwealth Group of Eminent Persons,* *Mission to South Africa*.[36] And in due course the Seven Against Pretoria met with the Secretary-General at Marlborough House in London in August 1986.† The Eminent Persons had been discomforted towards the end of their visit. When agreement had seemed near on a mode of dialogue, it was destroyed by a sudden attack by the South African air force on targets in Zambia, Zimbabwe and Botswana. The Committee also discovered that the National government under President P.W. Botha was obdurate. And that is certainly true. Afrikaners are not malleable, being born of different traditions, including distrust of the outside world. They are not springboks but pachyderms, distrustful of the West, and now by the visiting group distrusted. The report ends pessimistically, without any belief in Pretoria's ability to reform.

The report had less effect on South Africa than on the Commonwealth. Division ran deep between the six leaders and Mrs Thatcher, to the point of a divided communiqué. Its 17 paragraphs had to be interrupted by noting that Mrs Thatcher had agreed only to differ, her colleagues expressing 'both concern and regret that the British Government does not join in our agreement' on further

*The Eminent Persons were: Malcolm Fraser (Australia), General Olusegun Obasanjo (Nigeria), Lord Barber (Britain), Dame Nita Barrow (Barbados), John Malecela (Tanzania), Sardar Swaran Singh (India), The Most Rev. Edward Scott (Canada).
†Rajiv Gandhi, Bob Hawke, Kenneth Kaunda, Robert Mugabe, Brian Mulroney, Lynden Pindling, Margaret Thatcher.

measures (see Appendix D). Shridath Ramphal's attempt to mobilize the Commonwealth behind a single policy had not succeeded.

Mrs Thatcher did yield a little. Britain would accept, she said, a decision by the EEC if, when it met in September, it agreed to ban imports of iron, steel and coal from South Africa, although she added that 'she would not wish to defend the effect upon South African families'.[37] She was also prepared to accept a 'voluntary ban' – an odd combination – on new investment and tourist promotion. These were trivial concessions, and her fellow prime ministers were unimpressed. They took her to task and undertook to implement the full Nassau programme, plus three additional measures against bank loans, uranium, coal, steel and iron imports, and the withdrawal of consular facilities. They also agreed to 'look beyond the Commonwealth to the wider international community with a view to securing concerted action in the coming months'. Brave words, although the front-line states have not yet been able to live up to them.

f. VANCOUVER, 1987

The Commonwealth as a land of make-believe came fully into its own at the Heads of Government meeting held in Vancouver on 13–17 October 1987. While Western and Soviet naval forces were on armed alert in the Persian Gulf, and Indian soldiers were attacking Tamil strongholds at Jaffna in Sri Lanka, the Commonwealth settled down to arguments over Fiji and to renewed demands (on Britain) for sanctions against South Africa. The world might be lost in conflict, but the Heads of Government were not diverted. They were caught up in the past, and where better than among the fiords and mountains of British Columbia? Not far from the conference centre in Vancouver, the University Museum of Anthropology houses the carved totem-poles of the North American Indians, beguiled over the centuries by dreams from a past which failed to protect them; at the turn of the century, the census returns showed that their numbers had fallen to a quarter of the total population – 'at one time a dangerous element, they are now quiet and peaceable'. In October 1987 Commonwealth leaders assembled before their own totem-pole, meeting first in Vancouver, then at their retreat on the shores of Lake Okanagan.

They, too, were bemused. There had been every expectation of a quiet meeting. The phrase used by Shridath Ramphal for his *1987 Report to the Heads of Government* was 'A Time for Renewal'. Where Nassau had been torrid, it was hoped that Vancouver would be temperate: a period of calm after the storm. But there were spirits still to be appeased.

The islands of Fiji, a Commonwealth member since 1970, had become a problem. Colonel Rabuka's armed intervention and decision to declare a republic had its effect. After a good deal of hesitation, the Governor-General stood down, and by proclamation at Vancouver the Queen ceased to be Head of State for a former colony whose (Fijian) inhabitants had loyally served the Crown since 1874.

Alas, that it should have to be so. The coup which removed Fiji's elected government became entangled in an arcane web of procedure which went back to India's republican constitution of 1949–50. No matter that a majority of Commonwealth members were now republics, or that soldiers had set aside the constitution of Sierra Leone in 1967 when still under the Crown, of the Seychelles in 1977 during a Commonwealth conference in London, and of Grenada after a bloody revolt in 1979 The fact, too, that many Commonwealth countries have been worse offenders against human rights than Fiji was not considered. Colonel Rabuka offended protocol, not by abrogating the islands' constitution, but by declaring his intention to discriminate against Fiji's Indian population. He was therefore caught in the net that Commonwealth governments were still seeking to throw over South Africa. There lay the rub. The convention was that the declaration of a republic cancelled a country's membership; but it was also common practice that readmission followed. No member country had been refused hitherto, although South Africa declined in 1961 to reapply. The difficulty for Fiji lay in the Commonwealth's overriding concern with race. Those who were fiercely hostile towards apartheid could not publicly condone in the South Pacific what they condemned in South Africa.

Colonel Rabuka was worried not about South Africa but about the parallel situation, as he saw it, of the Kanak population in New Caledonia – now outnumbered by French settlers – and the Maori minority in New Zealand. He was not without support at Vancouver. Fiji's Melanesian neighbours were reluctant to take action; so was Malaysia, which fully understands the art of balancing minorities against a majority; Britain, too, preferred a 'wait-and-see' policy. But the rigidity of Commonwealth procedures could not be softened. And since readmission required unanimity, and since India was displeased, Fiji became a lapsed member – at best, in limbo. The islands are not the first to cease to belong – Eire, South Africa and Pakistan precede them – but Fiji is the first to forfeit membership against its own wishes. The result is that Commonwealth leaders will meet Fiji's new rulers in bodies like the South Pacific Forum but no longer, it seems, in Commonwealth gatherings. The Commonwealth is in thrall to its own totem of 'race' and will not, or cannot, break its bonds.

But it was South Africa that dominated the agenda. Mrs Thatcher was urged once more to endorse what she had already declined to accept – a tightening of existing sanctions against the Republic. There was no regard for arguments that Britain's EC partners, plus Japan and the United States, might be unwilling to follow, that indeed they were likely to take up any share of trade with southern Africa that had been forfeited by the United Kingdom. Morality was weighed against interests, and Britain was found wanting. There was open disagreement, therefore, at the daily press conferences and in the plenary sessions: Canada versus Britain in undignified dispute over trade statistics, Zambia versus Britain, India versus Britain, Zimbabwe versus Britain over the likely effect of sanctions and the morality of seeming to support apartheid. The argument spread into unlikely channels. Mrs Thatcher came close to endorsing Marxist beliefs that economics must necessarily triumph over politics: the South African economy, she said, would make nonsense in time of apartheid and sense even of National Party policy. Mr Mugabe seemed almost to forget that Zimbabwe and the front-line states had also backed away from implementing the full Nassau programme of sanctions.

The communiqué drafted at Lake Okanagan had to include the phrase 'with the exception of Britain' throughout its paragraphs (see Appendix E). 'Why parade our differences?' Mrs Thatcher had asked during her opening address. But since those who demanded action hardly knew what to do, and since the one country which had the capacity to act refused to comply, what else could the leaders do but disagree?

Vancouver, however, was not quite like Nassau. Although the leaders quarrelled down to the last press conference, it was not with a full heart. The rancour of earlier meetings was modified by lack of conviction. As the Canadian Foreign Minister remarked, members were 'sanctions-weary'. There were also areas of Commonwealth agreement. Britain and Canada undertook to increase their aid to member countries of SADCC (South African Development Coordination Conference), and to Mozambique – an observer at Vancouver – in particular. There was endorsement for a new Commonwealth University of the Air. There was a useful examination of the difficulties facing world trade, Third World debts and agriculture in the run-up to the Uruguay Round of the GATT. The communiqué also included a guarded statement on the accord between India and Sri Lanka, although events may yet make it nugatory.

The conference was brought to a close on 17 October. The prime ministers and presidents were escorted on their way by red-coated Mounties. The totem-poles stood silent in the Vancouver Museum. Mr Brian Mulroney, whose government had spent a great deal of money on the conference, refused to despair. 'There is much more to this institution', he declared, 'than one sometimes reads in the press. The Commonwealth, which often seems in danger of slipping apart, always finds a way of keeping the family unit together.' That most Commonwealth of figures, Mr Micawber, would have understood:

'My dear Copperfield', said Mr Micawber, 'accidents will occur in the best-regulated families . . . ; they may be expected with confidence, and must be borne with philosophy.'

* * *

The Commonwealth was undoubtedly wounded at Nassau and Vancouver. The spectre of apartheid reappeared, like Banquo's ghost, at successive meetings, shaking its gory locks and disturbing the guests. And since racial discrimination in South Africa is unlikely to be exorcized in the short or medium run, it remains a threat to Commonwealth unity. African member countries are hostile not only because Pretoria holds the front-line states hostage but because apartheid robs them of their own achievements. Western governments, too, are uneasy in that South Africa is a mirror to their conscience: they see reflected not what they are but what they might be if faced with South Africa's ill-fortune. Conflict between majority and minority communities pushed the North American Indians and the Australian Aborigines almost out of history; it disturbs New Zealand as much as Fiji, bids fair to keep Sri Lanka and India divided and threatens the unity of African states. None is free of its dangers. South Africa has been dealt an unlucky, almost unplayable, hand through the arithmetic of its racial make-up, and one must expect apartheid to continue to haunt Commonwealth gatherings.

Will the Commonwealth outlive white South Africa? Very probably, although whether the full tally of its present membership will be maintained is always open to doubt. The theme of these middle sections, however, has not been survival but change: metamorphosis. A transformation takes place and what was one thing becomes another. The story of Ovid's poem is that everything is altered by time – *tempus edax rerum* – and that has certainly been true of Commonwealth ties. An empire of enormous wealth and power has been transformed into an international association whose chief merit lies not in its capacity to act but in its willingness to argue.

3

BRITISH INTERESTS

What are British interests in the Commonwealth? Are they practical or sentimental? Are they a response to obligations from the colonial past, or do they constitute a framework of opportunity for the conduct of policy? The opening chapter of this essay argues that the Commonwealth has ceased to be an instrument for collective action outside a narrow range of uncontroversial issues; but does that mean there is no room for the adjustment of policy on the basis of Commonwealth agreements? And must the willingness to discuss always stop short of action? By 1987 the political temperature had dropped after the excitement of Nassau. One might reasonably say that the Commonwealth has reached a stage of 'qualified amiability'. But that does not answer the question of its utility.

Consider three broad questions. One is whether Commonwealth membership helps to smooth relations between governments, as between Britain and India or Britain and Nigeria. There is no simple answer, for if the colonial past has helped to establish friendly links, resentment of the past has also soured relationships. A second question: can the Commonwealth be used collectively, or must it always be seen as no more than a multiple set of bilateral relations? For example – and the matter is examined more closely later – overseas aid is a mixture of Commonwealth bilateral programmes, CFTC funding and grants allocated to Third World countries on the basis of greatest need. Is that a sensible mix? A third question: if the Commonwealth truly enhances Britain's standing in the world, what dangers would arise if it were to fracture, and how earnestly should Britain seek to keep the association in being?

Before looking at these questions, one must first be clear about the limits of British interests in any overall assessment of policy in 1987. There should be no room for ambiguity, and it may be helpful to restate here why the Commonwealth is now peripheral to British interests. The explanation is plain. For the rest of the decade and into the 1990s, policy has to follow two main assumptions. One is that neither the security nor the prosperity of the United Kingdom can be isolated from Western Europe, an assumption legally sealed in 1973. The other is that the decline of American power since the 1970s is likely to see the United States seeking agreements with the Soviet Union on defence, and on trade with Japan, which may run counter to European interests, and this too strengthens the need for priority to be given to European affairs. No longer part of that world of high national concern, the Commonwealth has to be seen as operating on the margin of British interests.

The association does, however, embrace a substantial segment of the world beyond Europe, Washington and Moscow. And since Britain's pattern of trade and investment is global, it must be in British interests to secure as peaceful and prosperous a community of nations as possible. No government, of any complexion, is likely to want to see the dismantling of links which at least try to keep alive a friendly international discourse. The choice, therefore, lies between maximum and minimum attention for Commonwealth affairs, whether Britain should move towards one position or the other, and how wide a margin of interest it should accord this curious post-colonial relationship.

There is a cheerful view which says that the time is appropriate for a strengthening of interest. It is broadly as follows. It admits that South Africa is still a difficulty, but argues that the air was cleared in 1985 when Mrs Thatcher made Britain's position clear without any break in membership. Recognition is growing that apartheid will not be ended, though it may be altered, by pressure from outside. Since what will happen in the Republic is absolutely beyond present knowledge, South Africa has to be categorized as one of the world's long-term problems. Meanwhile, the Commonwealth should look to its advantages. It has reached maturity. It has grown through a series of crises which tested the commitment, without destroying the resolve, of its members to stay together. There will be no more Rhodesia/Zimbabwe conflicts, few if any new members, no argument over regional versus Commonwealth priorities, and a better understanding of what the association can do. Leaders of the smaller member states look to Britain and the Commonwealth as the international organization in which their voice can best be heard, while for the larger countries (including Britain) the Commonwealth has become a sensible listening forum in which contacts are established, arguments tried out, grievances ventilated and programmes of help formulated. Without the warmth of such association the world would be a colder, more impersonal and diplomatically formal network of sovereign authorities. Britain should begin, therefore, to reclaim areas of joint interest and not turn its back on a period of history which is still a cause for pride. The time is ripe to act, but it will not be so forever. If the Commonwealth falls by neglect into disuse, no one will be able to retie its bonds of association.

The opposite argument is pessimistic and draws different conclusions, not from a belief that the time is ripe for change, but from the record of past hostility. Xenophobia rather than fraternity, and the decline of liberal beliefs, are said to be the hallmarks of the modern Commonwealth. The problem of racial conflict in southern Africa may have been pushed temporarily into the background, but who can doubt that it will return to the forefront of concern when the riots begin again, as they have done in the past – Sharpeville 1960, Soweto 1976, the townships in 1984–5 – and surely will again. Britain also has to have regard for the 800,000 British passport holders in the Republic: they too may become hostages to our fortune. Even if there is a tacit agreement at the next Heads of Government meeting to place South Africa on 'hold', the racial tension generated by apartheid will find new grievances in a range of issues: sport, immigration, medical screening, oil prices, trade restrictions. Other issues, of which Fiji at the Vancouver meeting was an example, will surely arise to impose further strain on the relationship. It would be prudent, therefore, to scale down the extent of our commitment, thereby freeing ourselves of a past which (as with nuclear weapons) exaggerates our status over our power. There is no strong sense of Commonwealth purpose that might act as a breakwater against the quarrels which will erode the association. Better, therefore, to minimize Britain's involvement. Then, if Nigeria or India or some other prominent member should quit, and if the domino effect of their leaving (as over the Edinburgh Games) reduces the Commonwealth to a residual body of fractured institutions, Britain will neither be harmed nor exposed to the blackmail of further threats to withdraw. Scale down! Fence in the Secretariat, prolong the interval between Heads of Government meetings, strengthen bilateral relations through the provision of aid, reduce subsidies to bodies like the Commonwealth Institute and do not differentiate between 'Commonwealth' and 'foreign'. Such decisions may seem peevish, but (so the argument concludes) they are actually prudent. If a tree is in danger of falling, why not shorten its branches and clear the ground beneath it?

Neither argument is compelling. Each exaggerates, the former by wanting too much, the latter by granting too little. Neither looks at the middle ground of moderate benefits.

The view from the high ground of optimism is admirably clear, but how can it be translated into policy? In July 1986 Neil Kinnock addressed the Royal Commonwealth Society. He too disliked existing attitudes. He believed that there had been a 'de-internationalization' of British interests, and he was convinced that 'active participation in the Commonwealth should be a central part of our modern foreign policy'.[1] Mr Kinnock was not specific, and very likely the occasion called forth the sentiment; but can there truly be a return to the days – which existed mainly in war – when the Commonwealth had a central role in British policy? For that to be possible Britain would either have to assume its former position of dominance, which is inconceivable, or run the danger of being used as an instrument of policy, which would be disagreeable. The truth is that, although the Commonwealth can usefully survey the world, it cannot take on its problems. No disparate array of sovereign states, geographically dispersed and with separate interests, could possibly do so unless it became what none of its members want it to be: an hierarchical organization of ordinary members and an inner council of the powerful, or a community of governments prepared to entrust executive decisions to a Commission or Secretariat. The proposal has only to be made to be dismissed. The Commonwealth was born to national sovereignty out of colonial dependence, and there is no going back on that.

The restrictive view, on the other hand, is too gloomy. It seeks to close down a past which is still sufficiently unpredictable to make one uncertain about its capacity to produce good or bad. The fact that the Commonwealth has moved away from the high noon of its post-war confidence to a more sober judgment of its worth does not

49

necessarily spell extinction. There is greater acceptance today, throughout the world of international relations, of the restraints on sovereignty and the limits to independence. There may therefore be room, among the Commonwealth's governments, for argument not only as a means to understanding but as the clearing-ground for agreement. Furthermore, as might be expected of an association fostered by British practice, the Commonwealth has muddled through a number of crises. For the present, therefore, it is wiser to postpone judgment and look more closely at the issues.

International policy

Should the leaders avoid high policy and focus on good deeds? No. If the Commonwealth is to have any *persona*, its prime ministers and presidents need to meet, and a two-yearly interval is probably about right. The world is changing: last year's problems, which seemed insurmountable, become this year's difficulties and more manageable. There are also long-running questions of international concern as sensible items for discussion – indebtedness, recession, inflation, terrorism, relations between Moscow and Washington, regional conflicts, immigration, drug-peddling and the new scourge of the Aids virus. The spread of membership gives an array of views and assembles a rich bank of information. The Commonwealth is unlike the meetings of francophone countries in this respect, and the coincidence of two conferences in 1987 at Vancouver (Commonwealth) and Quebec (Francophonie) ought not to be seen as too close a parallel. The ebb and flow of membership among French-speaking countries is not essential to the links between them: the Commonwealth is a formal organization for which the meetings between the leaders, in the presence of the Queen, are a necessary mark of its existence. One either is or is not a member. If at such conferences there is acceptance of the need to listen and explain, Britain will benefit, if only because Commonwealth membership still helps to complete the three circles of interest which, though they have changed their priorities, are still there.

Benefit in what sense? Can Britain expect unqualified support from Commonwealth governments? The answer is, clearly, no. There are too many differences of attitude and too many conflicts of interest. Can Britain count on substantial help during times of crisis? Perhaps, but here the past is a conflicting guide.

When policies were adopted by London that looked too much like imperialism, as at Suez in the mid-1950s, latent suspicions were awakened and Commonwealth governments were hostile. When a crisis moved into an acceptable framework, particularly that of decolonization, the response was favourable, as over Belize and – pre-eminently – Rhodesia. During 1979 and 1980, supportive votes at the UN, helpful intercessions by Tanzania, Zambia and other front-line states, together with observers in the field during the 1979 elections, all assisted Zimbabwe into full Commonwealth membership, an achievement very creditable to Mrs Thatcher's administration, which expressed its gratitude: what had been resented had become helpful.

Events of that kind seemed to belong to history, to part of the end of empire: in Seeley's words, the history of British rule overseas was 'closed up'. When the revolution in Grenada turned sour in 1983 and was overturned by US forces, Britain and the Commonwealth could do no more than look on. The United States was too powerful, Grenada too feckless. But history, even the history of colonial rule, was not quite over. It returned in unexpected guise in the south Atlantic and some of the lessons of that adventure are instructive.

General Galtieri's forces occupied the Falklands on 2 April 1982, and a Royal Naval Task Force sailed from Portsmouth forty-eight hours later to recover the islands. Despite long lines of supply and casualties inflicted by enemy aircraft, a beach-head was established at Port San Carlos on 21 May. Within a month of the landing, Major-General Jeremy Moore was able to accept the surrender, on 16 June, of 'all the Argentine armed forces in East and West Falklands together with their impediments'. In the words of the dispatch, the islands were 'once more under the government desired by their inhabitants'.

When the conflict began, many Commonwealth leaders were hesitant, but throughout May and June they were more helpful than not, particularly at the UN, where another kind of battle was fought. The degree of support varied. The New Zealand government offered a relief frigate for use in the Indian Ocean; most Commonwealth governments saw Argentina's invasion as aggression. Caribbean leaders were particularly opposed to Galtieri, bearing in mind the parallels with Guatemala and Belize, Venezuela and Guyana. What Britain did, it did alone; but, within the triple circle of support, the post-imperial relationship was as helpful, in what it could do, as the assistance given by Washington and Brussels.

The Falklands conflict was a singular event. In the ordinary routine of diplomacy, relations between Commonwealth countries are much like those between foreign states. They may sometimes be 'special', through the courtesy of established custom, and they are distinguished by changes of nomenclature (High Commissioners instead of Ambassadors, a Foreign and Commonwealth Office in London), but one should not read too much into such residual courtesies. The value of the Commonwealth connection arises when there is a coincidence of interests, and when friendly assumptions, based on language and practice, help to facilitate relationships. One can take two extreme instances at each end of a spectrum of involvement. (1) The present alarms in the Gulf lie in an area in which Commonwealth influence is virtually non-existent. That part of the world of 'informal empire' and British protectorates was never translated into Commonwealth. Britain acts alone or with the United States and (some) EC governments. (2) If, however, revolution were to engulf South Africa, the Commonwealth would be directly affected: there are seven member states within the region. They would need assistance; Britain, which is unlikely to be able to stand aloof, would need help over refugees, transit facilities, staging posts and joint diplomatic action. A 'Commonwealth solution' is improbable, but international mediation – even action – might very well involve both British and Commonwealth governments.

Over a range of issues between these two extremes Britain consults and informs its fellow members; it may properly expect some measure of sympathy when faced with particular problems. And these are not negligible assets. But the experience of recent conferences underlies the fact that, like other member governments, Britain may be attentive to Commonwealth advice but not at the expense of national priorities.

Economic problems

Similar conclusions can be drawn about economic issues. The French are often said to have maintained a firm grasp on their former colonies, although who actually pays the cost today of such support – France or the francophone states – is open to question. Britain cannot claim as much, and the Commonwealth has no such delusions. It has no overall economic policy, though it has an ample share of economic problems. Its leaders discuss, but cannot act. They can educate themselves about North-South relations, rich-poor dependencies, dollar deficits and EEC surpluses. They can look at the plight of states stricken by droughts or hurricanes or locusts. They can also inquire into the difficulties of particular commodities, problems of access to markets and the growth of inflationary pressures. Some of the hoped-for remedies, when discussed in full session or less formal meetings, may find their way into national policies. But the days of British-led collective attempts at rescue, of Ottawa Agreements, Empire Marketing Boards, sterling area preferences and Colombo plans are gone.

Commonwealth devotees point out that Commonwealth markets still account for over 20 per cent in value of Britain's overseas trade, but the figures are meaningless as a measure of advantage. They are the result, not of Commonwealth mechanisms for improvement, but of British businessmen toiling in world markets, some of which are located in Commonwealth countries. They are the reflection of Britain's historical relationship with its former colonies but not of Commonwealth ties as such. Indeed, the percentage of British trade with Commonwealth countries has been shrinking. The contrast can be seen in Britain and South Africa: trade increased after the Republic withdrew from the Commonwealth in 1961, and grew at a faster rate than with Australia or New Zealand. So did the rate of investment and the opening of subsidiary companies. In brief, the existence of the Commonwealth makes little difference to the pattern of British trade overseas, though most businessmen will admit to a preference for markets where English is spoken and the legal system is familiar. The 'neutrality' of Commonwealth markets can also be seen in the statistics of market share by other industrial nations – West Germany, Japan, the United States. They do not suggest that a 'Commonwealth factor' has any significance. In more abstract language, one can say that there exists no direct economic correspondence between a strong or weak commitment to Commonwealth issues and the scale of extracted benefits.

If trade and investment are global rather than post-imperial, what can be said of aid and technical assistance? Is the picture of an inert Commonwealth, largely irrelevant to the volume and direction of British trade, also true of the pattern of overseas aid? Should the government concentrate its programmes on Commonwealth countries? Should it also use multilateral agencies such as the CFTC to a greater or lesser degree?

The distribution of aid differs from the general economic picture to the extent that it is determined mainly by government, although associations like Oxfam and Christian Aid are important. Both government and charitable aid owe much to precedent and habit. Colonial rule determined where aid should go (the first Colonial Development and Welfare Act was in 1929, reinforced in 1943) and the pattern remains very similar today. The point is worth making to explain why it is that 60–70 per cent of all British bilateral aid and technical assistance goes to Commonwealth countries, a percentage which rises even higher if help to Pakistan and the Sudan is included. The direction is partly a deliberate choice, partly a combination of past and present factors – historical ties, familiarity of procedures and the belief that the funds granted will be well managed. The present has grown out of the past and is confirmed by practice. Voluntary agencies are similarly placed, although the plea of 'greatest need' has a stronger resonance, as when famine takes hold of the Sahel states or Ethiopia.

This description of overseas aid needs to be qualified in one important respect. In the harsh circumstances of the 1980s, governments began to insist on a reverse flow of advantage. In the fluffy words of government press reports (20 February 1980): 'We believe that it is right . . . to give greater weight in the allocation of our aid to political, industrial and commercial considerations alongside our basic development objectives.' The meaning was clear. Charity should show a return to its donors; or 'if we scratch your back, we expect to be soothed a little in return'. The result is that almost three-quarters of the aid given is not only on a bilateral footing but (according to the UK memorandum to the OECD in September 1981) 'tied to the procurement of British goods and services'. Given that requirement, one can understand why support for multilateral Commonwealth agencies – the CFTC in particular – is lukewarm. Moreover, the reluctance to surrender control is reinforced by the obligation on British governments to contribute to the multilateral European Development Fund, some of which of course goes to Commonwealth countries. The amount pledged to the CFTC – 'the exemplar of Commonwealth multilateral endeavours' – is small, and Ramphal's assertion that 'the resources provided to the Commonwealth Fund go further in terms of development assistance than they do through any other fund, bilateral or multilateral', is not generally accepted.[2]

Is current policy on aid misguided? Probably not. It is ungenerous. The allocations fall below the level that the government itself accepts as an internationally agreed percentage of national income. But without the reverse flow into 'British goods and services' – it was estimated that in the single month of October 1980 industry received almost £20 million from contracts under the aid programme[3] – it is difficult to believe that even the present amounts would be maintained. One may reasonably conclude, therefore, that the present provision of aid does strengthen Commonwealth links with Britain, but primarily on a country-to-country basis. Voluntary aid is not markedly different except that it is determined by particular needs: to many young people in Britain, and to the charitably minded, sympathy for the poor and afflicted paints a picture of 'the Third World' rather than of the Commonwealth as such.

A somewhat different image is shaped by the spread of interests below those of 'high policy'. It is in the exchange of people and ideas, at the junction of policy and popular interests, that Britain is often urged to be more 'Commonwealth-minded'; but the wish that it might be so is easier than the deed. Consider, for example, the movement of peoples in its most literal sense.

Migration

The migration of individuals and families is as old as mankind. We are still nomads. Today, however, would-be migrants travel by air and seek to cross the frontiers of sovereign states not only as huddled masses yearning to breathe free, but as the poor of one world looking for subsistence in another. The mechanisms of the market fail to work, since poverty in Britain and the squalor of its inner cities do not deter those who know much worse in their own societies. And air travel – so swift, so crowded, so heterogeneous in its human payloads – confronts the receiving authorities with the immediate problem of would-be immigrants, refugees, wives and dependants moving through customs alongside the familiar traffic of tourists, businessmen and returning citizens. As described earlier, acceptance of a unified Commonwealth citizenship after 1945 soon gave place to immigration controls. In the early decades, migration

outwards from Britain into Commonwealth and colonial territories
had been encouraged, but immigration was quite another matter.
Gone was the belief that 'Imperial overseas settlement, and the
interchange of populations between one part of the British Commonwealth and others is essential to the future happiness and
prosperity and even the survival of the British Empire'.[4] The door
that was open began to close and is now shut.

It is firmly closed in countries across the Commonwealth: Sri
Lanka against India, Nigeria against Ghana, the Caribbean islands
against each other, Australia against Asia, and Canada against any
would-be immigrant without specified skills. Compassion offers no
room to the poor, and controls in Britain have bordered on the
grotesque in the virginity tests of Indian women at Heathrow. The
change after Britain joined the European Communities 'produced a
remarkable situation at British airports, where those arriving for
disembarkation saw two sets of signs: "British and EEC Passports"
– the easy way – and "Commonwealth and Foreign Passports" –
signifying a tough time ahead.'[5] The situation was remarkable only
in relation to past expectations. Legislation after 1973 continued to
bar the way to new immigrants and to restrict entry for relatives (or
declared relatives) of those who had arrived before the barriers went
up. The policy is said to be popular, and party manifestos compete
with each other only over the manner in which controls should be
applied – compassionately (Labour), effectively (Conservative).

It may be popular, but is it sensible? The problem is actually wider
than the Commonwealth. The entire globe is over-populated, and
poor families are everywhere eager to move. The reservoirs are huge,
but must there be a blanket prohibition? Hugh Tinker has argued
for discrimination in the manner of discrimination: why treat all
countries alike? For some Commonwealth members emigration is
not simply a private choice but a public necessity. There are also
refugees from Commonwealth countries where human rights are
abused. If such a policy of discrimination were to be adopted, it
would not be new. As Tinker recalls, Malta was granted a quota
entry into Britain in the 1970s. Other Commonwealth governments
have exercised a similar discretion. The point is clearly made:

For India, Bangladesh, Nigeria, or any other large entities,
emigration is not really important as a solution to any of their
problems. Other strategies, such as freer trade or better com-

modity agreements offer much greater advantages. For the smaller territories, the so-called mini-states and micro-states, emigration is essential for survival.[6]

Here is a sensible if sensitive subject for Commonwealth inquiry. Heads of Government meetings in recent years have been reluctant to examine the question, although not shy of voicing their dislike of British policies. But since the advantage of the Commonwealth is its variety – rich and poor, large and small, populous and empty – there ought to be an opportunity for its leaders, without incurring charges of racism, sexism, tribalism or other disagreeable epithets, to combine compassion and realism and to inquire whether needs can be matched to a relaxation of controls in favour of some but not all member countries. The focus should be on the Commonwealth as a whole and not on British practice alone. The test would be whether the Commonwealth can take a collective view of problems which, if they cannot be solved, might at least be mitigated. The advantage to Britain would be a forum in which opinions and policies could be jointly discussed without the pressure of selected criticism.

Human rights and violation of democratic principles
A related difficulty. The Commonwealth still reflects something of its founding principles, which were those of a liberal parliamentary society. The beliefs it struggled to maintain were not simply those of Britain: the 1926 description – 'free institutions are its life blood' – was underwritten by Nehru and Senanayake as well as by leaders of the older Dominions. It is proper to ask, therefore, what has happened to this vision of the Commonwealth as an embodiment of parliamentary freedoms. Why do the present leaders tolerate gross breaches of what today are called human rights?

The answer is a muddle. Most governments, including Commonwealth military regimes, are like the poor cat in the adage, 'letting I dare not wait upon I would'. And the reason is plain. Either they are too fearful or there are too many villains among them, with the result that the EC, with its Court of Justice at Strasbourg, has eclipsed the Commonwealth.

The record of delay is long. Sir Dawda Jawara of the Gambia called for the setting up of a Commonwealth Commission on Human Rights at the Lusaka conference in 1979, and it was agreed to bring together a working party. The record of subsequent events was unfortunate, for Sir Dawda himself was forced to seek help from the Senegalese army the following year, when an attempted coup temporarily forced him out of office. President Hilla Limann, of Ghana – one of the countries which agreed to take part – was overthrown when Flight Lieutenant Rawlings intervened a second time at the end of December 1980. Nigeria, too, reverted to military rule. The proposals of the truncated committee were approved at the Melbourne conference, but by this time they had been whittled down to an agreement simply to establish a 'human rights unit' within the Secretariat. Even the working party's compromise suggestion of an Advisory Committee on Human Rights was deferred indefinitely, after being put to a meeting of Commonwealth law ministers in Colombo in 1983. The concept was then buried beneath a weight of earlier resolutions on racial discrimination, economic deprivation, social injustice, North-South differences and so forth – a depressing example of how well the Commonwealth can fudge when confronting the unpalatable.

The same obfuscation took place over Uganda. A Commonwealth team of observers was asked to monitor the 1980 elections – the first since 1962. They noted a number of 'imperfections and deficiencies', and expressed a 'deep unease', but then concluded that there had been 'a valid electoral exercise broadly reflecting the wishes of the people of Uganda'. Milton Obote was re-elected president, only to be ejected from office, and from Uganda, by Yoweri Museveni's Liberation Army.

Well, Uganda is a difficult country. But its leaders are not alone in their wickedness. Shridath Ramphal was now prepared to recognize that 'our world society is a less democratic place than it once promised to be', but in the *1977 Report of the Secretary-General* he concluded that the protection of human rights was 'an area fraught with difficulty' for the Commonwealth because of 'a long and necessary tradition of non-interference in the internal affairs of other states'. The way forward, he believed, was by calling on the Commonwealth 'to work for an ethic which constrains meddling but ... also inhibits excesses of the kind that demand and justify protest from without'. How that might be done was not examined, and the Secretary-General was in some difficulty himself, since he had no wish to see South Africa protected by any tradition of non-interference: apartheid, like Idi Amin's slaughter of his opponents, justified 'protest from without'. The Secretary-General was openly critical, therefore, of governments, Britain's in particular, which 'profess to lead the world in democratic values and fundamental freedoms' but which 'by the level of their economic involvement ... underwrite apartheid'. (Introduction to the *1985 Report of the Secretary-General.*)

The truth of the matter, however, is that the case against South Africa is substantially weakened by the blind eye turned towards the abuse of political and human rights in Commonwealth states. In Guyana, for example, the Secretary-General's own country, there is not only electoral malpractice but discrimination between Afro and Indian communities. The wrongdoing within Commonwealth countries does not mitigate the iniquities of Pretoria, but it does mock arguments for one man one vote, majority rule, freedom from arbitrary imprisonment and all the political rights denied by several Commonwealth governments to their own citizens.

What can be done? If the Commonwealth is no more than a residual meeting-ground for the good and the bad, brought together by the accident of history and the coincidence of empire, then nothing needs to be done. If, on the other hand, it is believed that 'free institutions' ought to be the hallmark of membership, then some form of monitoring should be welcomed. The second of a number of Commonwealth Principles drawn up and subscribed to by all Heads of Government at the Singapore conference in January 1971 runs: 'We believe in the liberty of the individual, in equal rights for all citizens regardless of race, colour, creed or political belief, and in their inalienable right to participate by means of free and democratic political processes in framing the society in which they live.'

Why not, therefore, re-examine Sir Dawda's 'Commonwealth Commission on Human Rights'? It would need independent finance. It would need to be kept away from the Secretariat, which is compromised by being the servant of all Commonwealth governments. Might it be prudent if proposals for reconsideration of such a body came from one of the smaller democratic members – New Zealand, Barbados, Botswana or Samoa? Its findings, like those of Amnesty International, might be embarrassing to Commonwealth governments which have bundled away parliaments and civil rights. But they might also do something, if only a little, to restore to the

Commonwealth an awareness of the political freedom it was once committed to uphold and is in danger of losing.

The unofficial Commonwealth

The title is loose, since it covers a number of government-funded training schemes and Commonwealth-financed institutions as well as voluntary-based societies and professionally sponsored associations. The array is impressive and a little daunting – a Magistrates Association, an Association of Tax Administrators, Commonwealth journalists, architects, librarians and museum curators, many of them under an umbrella body, funded by the Commonwealth Foundation, known as the 'Commonwealth Professional Association'. One wonders a little whether they are all truly needed. The parallel links formed by the Secretary-General with international bodies border on fantasy: 'agreements with Imco, Unesco, Unido, Unep and Habitat', like some strange language of the unknown.[7]

Accepting the need, and looking at the activities of the various societies, two characteristics stand out. One is that the boundary between the Commonwealth and the world in general is very fluid. There is often an overspill and sometimes a shift from predominantly Commonwealth to marginal Commonwealth interests. Just as immigrants arrive from Pakistan, Vietnam, Iran and Lebanon, and in much the same way as aid programmes include Ethiopia, Mozambique and the Sudan, so the area of voluntary organizations and training schemes goes beyond the Commonwealth. Administrators-in-training arrive from Mexico, Indonesia, the Philippines, Thailand. Arms sales are global, and the provision of military training brings in Mozambique as well as Uganda, and Oman alongside Kenya.

The shift can be substantial. The former Imperial Defence College in Belgrave Square – now the Royal College of Defence Studies – and the Royal Naval College at Greenwich always had a small number of non-Commonwealth officers. Today, however, the RCDS and Greenwich have a minority of Commonwealth representatives among those who attend from NATO countries, South America and the Far East. Similarly, youth groups which draw together young people from member countries are also linked to Boy Scouts, Boys Brigade, Girls Brigade and youth movements across the world. The list could be extended, and the reason for the overspill or change in the pattern of recruitment is simple: the Commonwealth is not always a satisfactory subdivision of the world. It is neither exclusively English-speaking (unlike the association of francophone countries, which defines itself by language) nor fully self-sufficient. The point has been made in various contexts. There is a Commonwealth Arts Association and an Arts Organization, but they have difficulty in finding a common element among musicians, cinema directors, graphic artists and dancers, who are either regionally located or able to operate in the world at large. The issue can be evaded by arguing that the Commonwealth is strongest when it is a catalyst or a link association with the wider world, but the defence is somewhat half-hearted.

The second characteristic confirms this lack of a 'pan-Commonwealth identity' and raises serious problems. Few intra-Commonwealth associations are politically or financially autonomous. They cannot build a Commonwealth base without funds. The lack of funds leads them to governments, and governments impose their will, bringing them back under national control. There is little money available from Commonwealth sources: 'the unofficial Commonwealth has in general been given the cold shoulder by the Secretariat and by Commonwealth governments'.[8] The most conspicuous example, not of neglect but of interference, has been in Commonwealth-sponsored sporting events, but there are numerous other examples when government policy has hindered the growth of a Commonwealth-wide sentiment. Educational links have always been important, but they are weaker today, not only because American influence is stronger, but because local universities are nationally conscious, and because governments insist on measures that cut down the movement of students and teachers. The raising of fees for overseas students in Britain, Australia and Canada undoubtedly diverted many who would have preferred to study within a Commonwealth 'community of learning', and it remains to be seen whether proposals for a new Commonwealth University of the Air will remedy the loss. The overall effect has meant that the Commonwealth is not as fecund as its supporters would like it to be. National governments itch to monitor, influence and control, and have hampered the growth of a freely associating pan-Commonwealth sentiment.

*   *   *

Why should one be surprised? National sovereignty is woven into Commonwealth history and has always been given precedence over any non-government, wholly Commonwealth endeavour. The hard rock of national independence is still the basis of cooperation. Such has been the 'teleology' of Commonwealth development. The paramountcy of national interests moved the Self-Governing Colonies towards statehood, dissolved a common allegiance and broke up the Central African and West Indian Federations; it dismembered the West African Currency Board, West African Airways, East African Airways and the East African Common Services Organization. Nationalism led Singapore to quit Malaysia, Pakistan to secede from India, and Bangladesh to break from Pakistan. The great paradox in the recent history of this Commonwealth of nations has been the way in which Britain, its founding member, has moved away from national sovereignty – yet how slowly and reluctantly! – into association with its European neighbours.

We are approaching the end of the story, and the evidence of the past forty years lends force to the argument that the Commonwealth has survived in very attenuated form. There has been a paring-down of achievement, and different possibilities await its leaders.

One is that the post-imperial Commonwealth may finally prove to have been transitory, extremely useful in easing the pain of separation but of failing consequence beyond that. The critical years were 1947–9, when India opted to stay within the Commonwealth and moved quickly towards republican status. There is little point in speculating what might have been the relationship between Britain and the Dominions had India and much of the colonial empire not accepted membership. There would very likely have been both loss and gain. The modern Commonwealth, however, dates from 1947 and the result has been an increasingly diverse association. Because successive Commonwealth conferences and the Secretariat were unable to reach any common ground of policy, they have moved sensibly with and not against the tide of national sentiment. But the effect is plain to see in a lack of coordination which (to alter the analogy) stunts new growth.

The question is whether this process of attenuation will continue and, if so, where it will end. Will there be a particular point of fracture, or simply a lack of support to keep the association in existence? One must recognize that the Commonwealth is vulnerable precisely because it commits its members at the highest level between governments. No state has withdrawn and rejoined, although Pakistan has expressed an interest in re-entry. Moreover, to end the relationship severs ties at many other levels. There is no half-way house.

The danger to British interests would be worst if the break came from anger over policy in London, as seemed to threaten in 1985–6. On the experience of previous crises, the effect on trade and investment can be damaging: the nationalization of oil company assets in Nigeria in protest against policy on Rhodesia; a 'Buy British Last' edict in Malaysia when overseas student fees were increased; and visa requirements by India because of differences over immigration policy. There have been times when it looked as if Commonwealth membership imposed penalties rather than benefits, and events in South Africa constantly threaten. Other members' quarrels may also lead to fracture, as happened between India and Pakistan. Such disputes do not directly affect British interests; but if the Commonwealth were critically weakened by the withdrawal of member countries, a sense of failure would cast its shadow across the association as a whole.

A second possibility is equally sombre, that of a decline in commitment and an indifference to Commonwealth concerns among its leading members. There have been past conferences when various Heads of Government declined to attend, either because of domestic problems or through lack of interest. No immediate harm is caused, but the long-term consequence might be a rump Commonwealth and a lumpen Secretariat. The need to tidy up what was left could also hurt Britain's interests, if not its pride, together with some lessening of its standing abroad.

In practice, neither outcome – fragmentation by crisis or decay through neglect – is certain. The association has lived through so many troubled years that the odds on its continued survival must be favourable. What does stand out today is that Britain has less cause than in the 1950s and 1960s to fear the effect of a weakening of Commonwealth ties. If a time should come when, sadly, 'there is a rift within the lute, so that by and by the music's mute', Britain will outlive the silence. Already a new chapter in its history has opened in Europe as the alternative to Little England or to Britain-without-Empire. If it has not found a role, Britain has at least secured a place, in a new venture.

63

British interests

No threat is implied to the Commonwealth, which has coexisted with Britain-in-Europe since 1973. The matter is essentially one of balance. From about the mid-1960s British-Commonwealth relations were soured by quarrels over central and southern Africa. Affection was marred by exasperation on both sides. But Britain is no longer engaged in disburdening itself of empire and, if the argument of this essay is right – that the Commonwealth is still a useful argumentative forum for all its governments, offering a place for small states to be heard, extending benefits (albeit on a modest scale) to its members, and providing opportunities for discussion of problems of common interest – then the balance of interest might usefully be moved back a little to the centre. No great turn of policy or shift in resources is needed. The change required is as much a question of attitude as of direction and of trust in the advantages of membership. For the Commonwealth to have reached a position of 'qualified amiability' among a third of the world's nation-states is no small achievement, and there are problems enough to engage its attention. If luck and judgment run together, there is no reason why a Britain which is confident of its place in Europe, and of its influence in the world at large, should not be able to keep its ties with the Commonwealth in sensible repair.

APPENDICES
Appendix A: Members of the Commonwealth

Country	Capital	Population 1982	Population density (sq km) 1982	Joined Commonwealth
Antigua & Barbuda	St John's	77,000	175	November 1981
Australia	Canberra	15,170,000	2	January 1931
Bahamas	Nassau	218,000	16	July 1973
Bangladesh	Dhaka	92,859,000	645	March 1972
Barbados	Bridgetown	258,000	599	November 1966
Belize	Belmopan	152,000	7	September 1981
Botswana	Gaborone	998,000	2	September 1966
Britain	London	56,280,000	231	
Brunei Darussalam	Bandar Seri Begawan	250,000	43	January 1984
Canada	Ottawa	24,600,000	2	July 1931
Cyprus	Nicosia	645,000	70	March 1961
Dominica	Roseau	80,000	107	November 1978
Fiji*	Suva	658,000	36	October 1970
The Gambia	Banjul	682,000	60	February 1965
Ghana	Accra	12,169,000	51	March 1957
Grenada	St George's	113,000	328	February 1974
Guyana	Georgetown	798,000	4	May 1966
India	New Delhi	716,985,000	218	January 1947
Jamaica	Kingston	2,217,000	202	August 1962
Kenya	Nairobi	18,115,000	31	December 1963
Kiribati	Tarawa	60,000	68	July 1979
Lesotho	Maseru	1,440,000	47	October 1966
Malawi	Lilongwe	6,452,000	54	July 1964
Malaysia	Kuala Lumpur	14,528,000	44	August 1957
Maldives	Malé	163,000	547	July 1982
Malta	Valletta	360,000	1,139	December 1964
Mauritius	Port Louis	985,000	528	March 1968
Nauru	Nauru	8,000	381	January 1968
New Zealand	Wellington	3,160,000	12	February 1931
Nigeria	Lagos	90,572,000	98	October 1960
Papua New Guinea	Port Moresby	3,128,000	7	September 1975
St Christopher-Nevis	Basseterre	53,000	197	September 1983
St Lucia	Castries	124,000	201	February 1979
St Vincent and the Grenadines	Kingstown	112,000	260	October 1979
Seychelles	Mahé	64,000	229	June 1976
Sierra Leone	Freetown	3,194,000	45	April 1961
Singapore	Singapore	2,471,000	4,253	October 1965
Solomon Islands	Honiara	245,000	9	July 1978
Sri lanka	Colombo	15,189,000	232	February 1948
Swaziland	Mbabane	664,000	38	September 1968

(continues on next page)

Appendix A (*concluded*)

Country	Capital	Population 1982	Population density (sq km) 1982	Joined Commonwealth
Tanzania	Dar es Salaam	19,763,000	21	December 1961
Tonga	Nuka'alofa	100,000	143	June 1970
Trinidad & Tobago	Port of Spain	1,128,000	220	August 1962
Tuvalu	Funafuti	8,000	289	October 1978
Uganda	Kampala	13,451,000	60	October 1962
Vanuatu	Port Vila	123,000	10	July 1980
Western Samoa	Apia	159,000	56	August 1970
Zambia	Lusaka	6,000,000	8	October 1964
Zimbabwe	Harare	7,500,000	19	April 1980

* Fiji is at present in limbo.

Appendix B: Rates of contribution to the Secretariat

Country	%	Contributions to Secretariat 1984/5 £	Contributions to CSC 1984/5 £	Pledges to CYP 1984/5 £	Pledges to CFTC 1984/5 £
Antigua & Barbuda	0.75	40,279			12,650
Australia	8.54	458,639	53,880	220,544	4,058,698
Bahamas	0.75	40,279	3,330	8,316	25,300
Bangladesh	1.50	80,557	3,330	5,385	90,201
Barbados	0.75	40,279	3,330	5,731	25,300
Belize	0.75	40,279			4,610
Botswana	0.75	40,279	3,330	2,015	69,000
Britain	30.00	1,611,147	87,780	413,070	6,607,000
Brunei Darussalam	0.75	40,279	100	2,000	25,300
Canada	16.76	900,093	53,880	413,070	8,284,628
Cyprus	0.75	40,279	3,330	997	22,800
Dominica	0.75	40,279		296	
Fiji	0.75	40,279		10,197	37,950
Gambia	0.75	40,279		5,000	
Ghana	1.50	80,557	3,330	1,184	23,000
Grenada	0.75	40,279	3,330	3,041	8,640
Guyana	0.75	40,279	3,330	6,325	50,000
India	1.95	104,724	26,940	49,415	230,878
Jamaica	1.50	80,557	3,330	2,413	120,010
Kenya	1.50	80,557	3,330	11,880	38,989
Kiribati	0.75	40,279		366	
Lesotho	0.75	40,279	3,330	2,937	12,650

(*continues on next page*)

Appendix B (concluded)

Country	Contributions to Secretariat 1984/5 %	Contributions to Secretariat 1984/5 £	Contributions to CSC 1984/5 £	Pledges to CYP 1984/5 £	Pledges to CFTC 1984/5 £
Malawi	0.75	40,279	3,330	3,963	12,500
Malaysia	1.50	80,557	3,330	15,000	50,000
Maldives		1,000		439	2,000
Malta	0.75	40,279	3,330	1,080	
Mauritius	0.75	40,279	3,330	1,200	22,150
Nauru		1,000			638
New Zealand	1.50	80,557	26,940	31,605	451,500
Nigeria	1.50	80,557	3,330	31,131	622,000
Papua New Guinea	1.50	80,557	3,330	3,297	87,110
Seychelles	0.75	40,279	3,330		6,325
Sierra Leone	1.50	80,557	3,330		
Singapore	1.50	80,557		2,200	10,000
Solomon Islands	0.75	40,279		1,210	
Sri Lanka	1.50	80,557	3,330	6,538	21,000
St Christopher-Nevis	0.75	40,279		154	1,500
St Lucia	0.75	40,279	100	1,892	6,900
St Vincent and the Grenadines		2,250		589	895
Swaziland	0.75	40,279	3,330	3,720	34,800
Tanzania	1.50	80,557	3,330		82,050
Tonga	0.75	40,279		237	11,400
Trinidad & Tobago	1.50	80,557	3,330	20,930	
Tuvalu		1,000		96	1,065
Uganda	1.50	80,557	3,330	105	38,720
Vanuatu	0.75	40,279			15,500
Western Samoa	0.75	40,279		763	12,650
Zambia	1.50	80,557	3,330	14,035	51,900
Zimbabwe	1.50	80,557	3,330	5,641	63,378
Bermuda					11,500
British Virgin Islands					6,650
Cayman Islands					1,600
Cook Islands				235	800
Hong Kong				2,000	45,000
Montserrat					650
TOTAL	100.00	5,375,740	336,200	1,312,242	21,419,785

Note: This table lists government contributions to the Secretariat, the Commonwealth Fund for Technical Co-operation (CFTC), the Commonwealth Youth Programme (CYP) and the Commonwealth Science Council (CSC). Governments make contributions to the budget of the Secretariat at the percentage rates shown in the first column, with special members paying a fixed sum. Countries which are members of the CSC also contribute to its budget on an agreed scale. The CFTC and the CYP are financed by voluntary subscriptions. The CFTC receives additional contributions from some member countries in respect of specific projects, and these are reflected in the Fund's accounts.
Source: Report of the Commonwealth Secretary-General 1985.

Appendix C: The Commonwealth Accord on Southern Africa, Lyford Cay, Nassau, 20 October 1985

1. We consider that South Africa's continuing refusal to dismantle apartheid, its illegal occupation of Namibia, and its aggression against its neighbours constitute a serious challenge to the values and principles of the Commonwealth, a challenge which Commonwealth countries cannot ignore. At New Delhi we expressed the view that 'only the eradication of apartheid and the establishment of majority rule on the basis of free and fair exercise of universal adult suffrage by all the people in a united and non-fragmented South Africa can lead to a just and lasting solution of the explosive situation prevailing in Southern Africa'. We are united in the belief that reliance on the range of pressures adopted so far has not resulted in the fundamental changes we have sought over many years. The growing crisis and intensified repression in South Africa mean that apartheid must be dismantled now if a greater tragedy is to be averted, and that concerted pressure must be brought to bear to achieve that end. We consider that the situation calls for urgent practical steps.

2. We, therefore, call on the authorities in Pretoria for the following steps to be taken in a genuine manner and as a matter of urgency:

(a) Declare that the system of apartheid will be dismantled and specific and meaningful action taken in fulfilment of that intent.

(b) Terminate the existing state of emergency.

(c) Release immediately and unconditionally Nelson Mandela and all others imprisoned and detained for their opposition to apartheid.

(d) Establish political freedom and specifically lift the existing ban on the African National Congress and other political parties.

(e) Initiate, in the context of a suspension of violence on all sides, a process of dialogue across lines of colour, politics and religion, with a view to establishing a non-racial and representative government.

3. We have agreed on a number of measures which have as their rationale impressing on the authorities in Pretoria the compelling urgency of dismantling apartheid and erecting the structures of democracy in South Africa. The latter, in particular, demands a process of dialogue involving the true representatives of the majority black population of South Africa. We believe that we must do all we can to assist that process, while recognizing that the forms of political settlement in South Africa are for the people of that country – all the people – to determine.

4. To this end, we have decided to establish a small group of eminent Commonwealth persons to encourage through all practicable ways the evolution of that necessary process of political dialogue. We are not unmindful of the difficulties such an effort will encounter, including the possibility of initial rejection by the South African authorities, but we

believe it to be our duty to leave nothing undone that might contribute to peaceful change in South Africa and avoid the dreadful prospect of violent conflict that looms over South Africa, threatening people of all races in the country, and the peace and stability of the entire Southern Africa region.

5. We are asking the President of Zambia and the Prime Ministers of Australia, The Bahamas, Canada, India, the United Kingdom and Zimbabwe to develop with the Secretary-General the modalities of this effort to assist the process of political dialogue in South Africa. We would look to the group of eminent persons to seek to facilitate the processes of dialogue referred to in paragraph 2(e) above and by all practicable means to advance the fulfilment of the objectives of this Accord.

6. For our part, we have as an earnest of our opposition to apartheid, reached accord on a programme of common action as follows:

(i) We declare the Commonwealth's support for the strictest enforcement of the mandatory arms embargo against South Africa, in accordance with United Nations Security Council Resolutions 418 and 558, and commit ourselves to prosecute violators to the fullest extent of the law.

(ii) We reaffirm the Gleneagles Declaration of 1977, which called upon Commonwealth members to take every practical step to discourage sporting contacts with South Africa.

(iii) We agree upon, and commend to other governments, the adoption of the following further economic measures against South Africa, which have already been adopted by a number of member countries:

(a) a ban on all new government loans to the Government of South Africa and its agencies;

(b) a readiness to take unilaterally what action may be possible to preclude the import of Krugerrands;

(c) no Government funding for trade missions to South Africa or for participation in exhibitions and trade fairs in South Africa;

(d) a ban on the sale and export of computer equipment capable of use by South African military forces, police or security forces;

(e) a ban on new contracts for the sale and export of nuclear goods, materials and technology to South Africa;

(f) a ban on the sale and export of oil to South Africa;

(g) a strict and rigorously controlled embargo on imports of arms, ammunition, military vehicles and paramilitary equipment from South Africa;

(h) an embargo on all military cooperation with South Africa; and

(i) discouragement of all cultural and scientific events except where these contribute towards the ending of apartheid or have no possible role in promoting it.

7. It is our hope that the process and measures we have agreed upon will help to bring about concrete progress towards the objectives stated above in

six months. The Heads of Government mentioned in paragraph 5 above, or their representatives, will then meet to review the situation. If in their opinion adequate progress has not been made within this period, we agree to consider the adoption of further measures. Some of us would, in that event, consider the following steps among others:

(a) a ban on air links with South Africa;

(b) a ban on new investment or reinvestment of profits earned in South Africa;

(c) a ban on the import of agricultural products from South Africa;

(d) the termination of double taxation agreements with South Africa;

(e) the termination of all government assistance to investment in, and trade with, South Africa;

(f) a ban on all government procurement in South Africa;

(g) a ban on government contracts with majority-owned South African companies;

(h) a ban on the promotion of tourism to South Africa.

8. Finally, we agree that should all of the above measures fail to produce the desired results within a reasonable period, further effective measures will have to be considered. Many of us have either taken or are prepared to take measures which go beyond those listed above, and each of us will pursue the objectives of this Accord in all the ways and through all appropriate fora open to us. We believe, however, that in pursuing this programme jointly, we enlarge the prospects of an orderly transition to social, economic and political justice in South Africa and peace and stability in the Southern Africa region as a whole.

Appendix D: Commonwealth Heads of Government Review Meeting, London, 3–5 August 1986, communiqué

1. As agreed at Nassau last October, our meeting was held in the special context of the crisis in Southern Africa. At the outset of our discussion we specifically reaffirmed our commitment to the Commonwealth Accord on Southern Africa which, with our other colleagues, we had concluded at Nassau. We reaffirmed, in particular, the united belief we expressed in the Accord that 'apartheid must be dismantled now if a greater tragedy is to be averted, and that concerted pressure must be brought to bear to achieve that end'.

2. At our request the Co-Chairmen of the Commonwealth Group of Eminent Persons (EPG), General Olusegun Obasanjo and Mr Malcolm Fraser, introduced the report of the EPG and answered the many questions we put to them. Sir Geoffrey Howe, the British Foreign Secretary, who undertook a mission to Southern Africa in his capacity as President of the Council of Ministers of the EEC, also briefed us on the results of his mission.

3. The Report of the EPG, *Mission to South Africa*, was the central document at our discussions. That unanimous Report has commanded attention worldwide as pointing the way forward for South Africa and for the world in relation to South Africa. We warmly commend the Group's work, which has made a positive and enduring contribution to the efforts to end apartheid and establish a non-racial and representative Government in South Africa. We particularly commend the EPG's 'negotiating concept' and deeply regret its rejection by the South African Government.

4. At Nassau, the Commonwealth unanimously adopted a common programme of action which included a number of economic measures against South Africa. It was our collective hope that those measures and the efforts of the EPG to promote a process of dialogue in South Africa would, within six months, bring about concrete progress towards our objectives of seeing apartheid dismantled and the structures of democracy erected in South Africa.

5. As envisaged in the Accord, we have reviewed the situation. We are profoundly disappointed that the authorities in Pretoria have taken none of the five steps which at Nassau we called on them to take 'in a genuine manner and as a matter of urgency'. Nelson Mandela and other political leaders remain in prison. A new and more widely repressive emergency has been imposed and political freedom more rigorously curtailed; the ANC and other political parties are still banned. Beyond these, however, it has been a matter of deep concern to us that the EPG after its most patient efforts has been forced to conclude that 'at present there is no genuine intention on the part of the South African Government to dismantle apartheid' and 'no present prospect of a process of dialogue leading to the establishment of a non-racial and representative government'. We had looked at Nassau for the initiation by Pretoria of a process of dialogue in the context of a suspension of violence on all sides. Instead, as the EPG found, the cycle of violence and counter-violence has spiralled.

6. We receive the Group's findings with disappointment, and deplore the conduct of the South African Government, whose actions, including the raids on neighbouring countries at a crucial moment of the EPG's work, terminated its efforts for peaceful change. We continue to believe with the EPG that the cycle of violence in South Africa must end. It is clearly established that the situation in South Africa constitutes a serious threat to regional peace and security.

7. It is thus clear to us that since our meeting in Nassau there has not been the adequate concrete progress that we looked for there. Indeed, the situation has deteriorated.

8. Accordingly, in the light of our review and of our agreement at Nassau, we have considered the adoption of further measures against the background of the EPG's conclusion that the absence of effective economic

pressure on South Africa and the belief of the South African authorities that it need not be feared are actually deferring change. We acknowledge that the Commonwealth cannot stand by and allow the cycle of violence to spiral, but must take effective concerted action.

9. We are agreed that one element of such action must be the adoption of further measures designed to impress on the authorities in Pretoria the compelling urgency of dismantling apartheid and erecting the structures of democracy in South Africa.

10. In doing so, we have looked particularly at the measures listed in paragraph 7 of the Accord, which some of us at Nassau had already indicated a willingness to include in any consideration of further measures. But we have looked as well to other measures under consideration elsewhere. In deciding on the adoption of further measures, we recognize that if they are to have maximum effect they should be part of a wider programme of international action.

11. The British Government's position is set out in paragraph 12. The rest of us have agreed as follows:

(a) The adoption of further substantial economic measures against South Africa is a moral and political imperative to which a positive response can no longer be deferred.

(b) We ourselves will therefore adopt the following measures and commend them to the rest of the Commonwealth and the wider international community for urgent adoption and implementation:

  (i) All the measures listed in paragraph 7 of the Nassau Accord, namely:
- a ban on air links with South Africa;
- a ban on new investment or reinvestment of profits earned in South Africa;
- a ban on the import of agricultural products from South Africa;
- the termination of double taxation agreements with South Africa;
- the termination of all government assistance to investment in, and trade with, South Africa;
- a ban on all government procurement in South Africa;
- a ban on government contracts with majority-owned South African companies;
- a ban on the promotion of tourism to South Africa.

  (ii) the following additional measures:
- a ban on all new bank loans to South Africa, whether to the public or private sectors;
- a ban on the import of uranium, coal, iron and steel from South Africa;
- the withdrawal of all consular facilities in South Africa except for our own nationals of third countries to whom we render consular services.

(c) While expressing both concern and regret that the British Government does not join in our agreement, we note its intention to proceed with the measures mentioned in paragraph 12 below.

(d) We feel, however, that we must do more. We look beyond the Commonwealth to the wider international community. We will, therefore, immediately embark on intensive consultations within the international community with a view to securing concerted international action in the coming months, our emphasis being on those countries that presently sustain a significant level of economic relations with South Africa.

12. The British Government, while taking a different view on the likely impact of economic sanctions, declares that it will:

   put a voluntary ban on new investment in South Africa;

   – put a voluntary ban on the promotion of tourism to South Africa; and

   – accept and implement any EEC decision to ban the import of coal, iron and steel and of gold coins from South Africa.

13. As a further element of our collective commitment to effective action, we have requested the Secretary-General, with assistance from our Governments, to coordinate the implementation of the agreed measures and to identify such adjustment as may be necessary in Commonwealth countries affected by them.

14. We renew the call we made at Nassau on the authorities in Pretoria to initiate, in the context of a suspension of violence on all sides, a process of dialogue across lines of colour, politics and religion with a view to establishing a non-racial and representative government in a united and non-fragmented South Africa. If Pretoria responds positively to this call and takes the other steps for which we called in paragraph 2 of the Nassau Accord, we stand ready to review the situation and to rescind the measures we have adopted if appropriate; and to contribute, in all ways open to us, to an orderly transition to social, economic and political justice in South Africa and to peace and stability in Southern Africa as a whole.

15. On the other hand, we are equally mindful of our further commitment at Nassau that if in a reasonable time even these further measures have not had the desired effect, still further effective measures will have to be considered. We trust that the authorities in Pretoria will recognize the seriousness of our resolve. Acts of economic or other aggression against neighbouring states by way of retaliation or otherwise will activate that resolve.

16. Regretting the absence of full agreement but recognizing that the potential for united Commonwealth action still exists, we agree that the seven Governments will keep the situation under review with the view to advising whether any further collective Commonwealth action, including a full Heads of Government meeting, is desirable. We are conscious that the

situation in South Africa may evolve rapidly and dangerously. We believe the Commonwealth must retain its capacity to help to advance the objectives of the Nassau Accord and be ready to use all the means at its disposal to do so.

17. Meeting in London at the time of heightened strains within our association, we take the opportunity to renew our own firm commitment to the future of the Commonwealth and to the aims and objectives which have guided it over the years. We are fortified in this renewal by the spirit of frankness in friendship which characterized our discussions and our belief that they have helped to light a common path towards fulfilment of our common purpose, namely, the dismantling of apartheid and the establishment of a non-racial and representative government in South Africa as a matter of compelling urgency.

Appendix E: Vancouver meeting, 13–17 October 1987, summary of main decisions

The following extract from *The Times* (19.x.87) summarizes three papers attached to the conference communiqué.

Vancouver Declaration on World Trade

The leaders noted with grave concern rising protectionist trends. Trade restrictions affect particularly the exports and growth prospects of developing countries and their ability to service debt.

The leaders agreed on the crucial need for reform of trade-distorting agricultural policies, and urged early action on agriculture in the Uruguay round of the General Agreement on Tariffs and Trade negotiations.

They hoped that the negotiations would make sufficient progress on agriculture and other key subjects to enable a mid-term ministerial review of the Uruguay round.

The Okanagan Statement on Southern Africa

The leaders reaffirmed their shared responsibility to work together for the total eradication of apartheid, and agreed that the urgency for international action had heightened.

They reaffirmed their commitment to the Commonwealth Accord on Southern Africa, reached at their previous meeting at Nassau. The leaders said that the rejection by Pretoria of the 'negotiating concept', submitted by the Eminent Persons' Group, was 'nothing less than a tragedy'.

The leaders remained convinced that catastrophe could only be averted through negotiations.

With the exception of Britain, the leaders believed sanctions had had significant effect. Wider, tighter and more intensified application must remain part of the international response to apartheid. With the exception of Britain, the leaders believed genuine efforts should be made to secure universal adoption of measures adopted by Commonwealth and other countries.

With the exception of Britain, they will initiate an expert study of South Africa's relationship with the international financial system.

The leaders agreed to continue to take further action individually and collectively. With the exception of Britain, this includes sanctions.

They decided to initiate an enhanced programme of coordinated Commonwealth assistance to the frontline states, particularly Mozambique.

Priority was to be given to the Limpopo railway line and the port of Maputo.

The Commonwealth would give support to opponents of apartheid in South Africa, to help victims of apartheid, to expand educational opportunities, to give humanitarian and legal assistance for detainees, to increase support for trade unions in South Africa, and to take any opportunity to promote dialogue with Pretoria.

The Commonwealth would give high priority to counteracting South Africa's presence in Namibia, and remained convinced that United Nations Resolution 435 was the only basis for settlement.

With the exception of Britain, the leaders agreed to set up a committee of foreign ministers to provide high-level impetus and guidance on anti-apartheid measures.

The leaders believed that some Commonwealth countries which have not previously been able to contribute to multilateral efforts on apartheid will now be able to do so.

The Commonwealth Secretary-General was to initiate consultations between donor and recipient countries.

Statement on Fiji

The leaders acknowledged that, on the basis of Commonwealth conventions, Fiji's membership had lapsed with the emergence of a republic on October 15.

They viewed developments in Fiji with sadness, and hoped for a resolution consistent with Commonwealth principles.

The leaders would, if requested, be ready to offer good offices towards resolution and, on such basis, to consider the question of Fiji's (renewed) membership, if so asked.

Sri Lanka

The Commonwealth communiqué also contained this passage on Sri Lanka:

The Heads of Government welcomed the Indo-Sri Lanka agreement, recently signed by the President of Sri Lanka and the Prime Minister of India, as an act of the highest statesmanship.

They were happy to note that the agreement meets with the legitimate aspirations of all the people in Sri Lanka within a democratic system of governance. It brings to an end the ethnic violence in Sri Lanka, restores peace and normalcy, and ensures the unity, integrity and stability of the country.

The Heads of Government acclaimed the agreement as one arrived at bilaterally between two member states of the Commonwealth in a spirit of understanding and accommodation which will ensure regional peace and stability.

The Heads of Government wished the two leaders every success in the full implementation of the agreement.

They affirmed their fullest support for the territorial integrity, independence and sovereignty of Sri Lanka.

NOTES

Foreword

1 'And when they came to Nachon's threshing floor, Uzzah put forth his hand to the ark of God, and took hold of it; for the oxen shook it. And the anger of the Lord was kindled against Uzzah; and God smote him there for his error, and there he died' (2 Sam. 6).

2 R. Stankiewicz, *British Government in an Era of Reform* (London: Macmillan, 1976).

3 Subsequently published: Prosser Gifford and Roger Louis, eds, *The Transfer of Power in Africa* (Yale: Yale University Press, 1982).

4 Hugh Tinker, *Experiment with Freedom* (London: Oxford University Press, 1967), p. 164.

5 Phrases used in the (Moyne) *West Indian Royal Commission, 1938–39* (London: HMSO, 1939), Cmd 6174, and in numerous colonial reports throughout the Empire.

6 W.K. Hancock, *Survey of British Commonwealth Affairs* (London: Oxford University Press, 1937), vol. 1, p. 61.

7 *Ibid.*, vol. 1, p. 61. The words quoted were from Cmd 2769 of 1926, p. 31.

8 R.G. Collingwood, *Speculum Mentis* (Oxford: Clarendon Press, 1924), p. 82.

Chapter 1

1 For the full quotation, see the 'High noon' section of Chapter 2.

2 Sir Robert Menzies, *Afternoon Light* (London: Cassell, 1967), p. 189.

3 'The Prince had always liked his London when it came to him; he was one of the modern Romans who found by the Thames a more convincing image of the ancient state than any they have left by the Tiber. Brought up on the legend of the City to which the world brought tribute, he recognized in the present London much more than in contemporary Rome the real dimensions of such a case.' Henry James, *The Golden Bowl* (New York: Doubleday, 1907), p. 3.

4 Kipling's *Kim* and Rider Haggard's *King Solomon's Mines* do not glorify colonial rule but are unintelligible without the background of Empire. Now of course 'the Rudyards have ceased from Kipling and the Haggards ride no more'.

5 The full text of the Report of the Inter-Imperial Relations Committee, Imperial Conference 1926, and the subsequent Statute of Westminster, which gave legal force in 1931 to its resolutions, may be found in Arthur Berriedale Keith, *Speeches and Documents on the British Dominions, 1918–1931* (London: Oxford University Press, 1932).

6 World Commission on Environment and Development, *Our Common Future* (Oxford University Press, 1987).

7 Nicholas Mansergh, *The Commonwealth Experience* (London: Weidenfeld & Nicolson, 1969), vol. 2, p 37.

8 *A Testing Time* (London: Commonwealth Secretariat, 1985), p. 21. This is the Introduction to the 1985 *Report of the Commonwealth Secretary-General*, which was issued as a separate publication.

9 Mrs Thatcher, *Address to the Commonwealth Parliamentary Association, September 1986*.

10 G.V. Desani, *All About H. Hatterr* (Harmondsworth: Penguin Books, 1972), p. 27.

Chapter 2

1 See particularly, Sir Keith Hancock, *Survey of British Commonwealth Affairs* (London: Oxford University Press 1937).

2 *The Blast of War* (London: Macmillan, 1967), p. 324.

3 Sir John Seeley, *The Expansion of England* (London, Macmillan, 1883). 'Some countries, such as Holland and Sweden, might presumably regard their history as in a manner wound up.'

4 *Parl. Deb.*, vol. 450, cols. 1316–1319.

5 *Ibid.*, cols. 1782–1795.

6 *The Commonwealth of Nations* (London: Oxford University Press, 1948), pp. 27–8.

7 The analogy used by Duncan Sandys in his account of *The Modern Commonwealth* (London: HMSO, 1962), p. 7: Empire at the top,

Commonwealth below, Her Majesty's Government in London being the filter from one to the other.

8 *The Times*, 12 March 1949.

9 Speech to the Indian Constituent Assembly. Quoted in Mansergh, *Survey of British Commonwealth Affairs . . . 1939–52* (London: Oxford University Press, 1958), p. 253.

10 E.g. A.A. Afrifa, who helped to lead the 1966 Ghana coup: 'One of the reasons for my bitterness against Kwame Nkrumah was that he paid lip service to our membership of the Commonwealth of Nations and proceeded to undermine the bonds that bind us in this great union of all races, colours and creeds.' And: 'To this end we belong to the British Commonwealth where, with millions of our fellow members of every creed and colour, and drawing on a common reservoir of wisdom and understanding, we can work towards our common goal of peace and prosperity' (Kenneth Kaunda, *Independence and Beyond*, London: Nelson, 1966). Also: 'Tanganyika's desire to join the Commonwealth hardly needs explanation. Our nationalism is not exclusive; we seek to promote African unity but not African isolation' (Julius Nyerere, *Uhuru na Umoju: Freedom and Unity, A selection of Writings and Speeches, 1952–65* (London: Oxford University Press, 1967).

11 See Dennis Austin, *Malta and the End of Empire* (London: Cass, 1971).

12 The only exception was Aden in 1967. An inglorious end to a troubled hinterland and a bankrupt coaling station.

13 See Lord Avon, *Full Circle* (Boston: Houghton, Mifflin, Company, 1965, p. 274): 'The failure to consult the US and the Commonwealth troubled us greatly . . . but the Indian reaction was remarkable. Mr Nehru declared . . . that whereas in Egypt "every single thing that had happened was as clear as daylight" he could not follow the very confusing situation in Hungary.' See, too, James Eayrs, *The Commonwealth and Suez, A Documentary Survey* (London: Oxford University Press, 1964).

14 'One of the pillars of our foreign policy is to fight against racial discrimination [but] it was a dangerous thing for us to bring that matter within the purview of the Commonwealth. Because then the very thing to which we object might have taken place. That is, the Commonwealth might have been considered as some kind of superior body which sometimes acts as a tribunal, or judges, or in a sense supervises the activities of its member nations. That would have meant a diminution in our independence and sovereignty . . . We are not prepared even to bring disputes between member nations before the Commonwealth body.' Nehru's worry was not South Africa but

Kashmir. Speech to the Constituent Assembly, 16 May 1949; quoted in Nandhini Iyer, *India in the Commonwealth* (New Delhi: ABC Publishing House, 1983), p. 65.

15 Roy Jenkins in Jenkins and Douglas Jay, *The Common Market Debate* (London: Fabian Publications, Tract no. 341, 1962).

16 Nicholas Deakin, 'Citizens and Immigrants into Britain', *Round Table*, April 1971.

17 Duncan Sandys, *The Modern Commonwealth* (London: HMSO, 1962), p. 5.

18 *The Times*, 10 May 1962.

19 *Ibid.*, 15 October 1962.

20 *Ibid.*, 2 October 1962.

21 'A Commonwealth of Learning', W.H. Morris Jones and T.J. Johnson, *Round Table*, November 1970.

22 *Round Table*, October 1971.

23 Speech at the Military Academy, West Point, January 1962.

24 There is still a list of dependent and semi-dependent territories: UK – Anguilla, Bermuda, British Virgin Islands, Cayman Islands, Falklands, Gibraltar, Hong Kong, Montserrat, Pitcairn, St Helena, Turks and Caicos. New Zealand controls the Tokelau and the self-governing states of the Cook Islands and Niue. Australian territories include Norfolk Island, Heard Island, McDonald Island, Cocos (Keeling) Island and Christmas Island.

25 *Report of the Review Committee on Overseas Representation, 1968–69* (London: HMSO, 1969), Cmnd 4107. (The Chairman was Sir Val Duncan.)

26 Andrew Shonfield, 'The Duncan Report and its Critics', *International Affairs*, April 1970.

27 *Canberra Notes*, September-October, 1972.

28 J.L. Granatstein, *Canada, 1957–67*, Canadian Centenary Services (Toronto: Mclelland and Stewart, 1986).

29 *The Times*, 7 August 1973.

30 Quoted in Arnold Smith and Clyde Sanger, *Stitches in Time: The Commonwealth in World Politics* (London: André Deutsch, 1981), p. 271.

31 A.J.R. Groom and Paul Taylor, *The Commonwealth in the 1980s* (London: Macmillan, 1984), p. 190.

32 *Ibid.*, p. 187.

33 See 'Sport and Apartheid', SANROC, *Newsletter*, London, various issues.

34 The inhabitants are democratic today – perhaps excessively so. At the close of the Heads of Government meeting, Sir Lynden Pindling, prime minister and host, was confronted by his opponents armed with

placards: 'The Chief is a Thief', 'Pindling the Black Botha', 'Pindling Apartheid'. They could not, however, prevent his re-election for a sixth term of office in 1987.

35 *The Annual Register for 1985*, p. 328.
36 Published by Penguin Books, 1986.
37 *The Times*, 10 August 1986.

Chapter 3

1 *The Commonwealth Today* (London: Commonwealth Secretariat, 1985), p. 14.
2 Quotations from Ramphal, *A Testing Time* (as ch.1, n. 8), p. 14.
3 See Groom and Taylor, *op. cit.*, p. 251.
4 Lord Cranbourne, 1943; quoted in *Migration Within the British Commonwealth* (London: HMSO, 1945), Cmd 6658.
5 Hugh Tinker, in Groom and Taylor, *op. cit.*, p. 252.
6 *Ibid.*, p. 256.
7 *The Commonwealth Today*, 1985, p. 14.
8 *Op. cit.*, p. 191.

BIBLIOGRAPHY

Books

Aiyar, S.P. *The Commonwealth in South Asia*, Bombay, Lalvani, 1969.

Austin, D. *Malta and the End of Empire*, London, Cass, 1971.

Austin, D. *South Africa 1984*, London, Routledge & Kegan Paul, for the Royal Institute of International Affairs, 1985.

Beloff, M. *Britain's Liberal Empire, 1897–1921*, London, Methuen, 1969.

Clarke, C., and Payne, A.J. *Politics, Security and Development in Small States*, London, Allen & Unwin, 1987.

de Silva, K.M. *Managing Ethnic Tension: Sri Lanka, 1880–1985*, New York, University Press of America, 1986.

Eayrs, J. *The Commonwealth and Suez, A Documentary Survey*, London, Oxford University Press, 1964.

Fischer G., and Morris-Jones, W.H. *Decolonisation and After*, London, Cass, 1980.

Garner, J. *The Commonwealth Office, 1925–1968*, London, Heinemann, 1978.

Gifford, P., and Louis, W.R. *The Transfer of Power in Africa: Decolonization 1940–1960*, Newhaven, Yale University Press, 1982.

Groom, A.J.R., and Taylor, P. *The Commonwealth in the 1980s*, London, Macmillan, 1984.

Hancock, W.K. *Survey of British Commonwealth Affairs*, vols 1 and 2, London, Oxford University Press, 1942.

Holland, R.F. *Britain and the Commonwealth Alliance, 1918–1939*, London, Macmillan, 1980.

Ingram, D. *The Imperfect Commonwealth*, London, Rex Collings, 1977.

Iyer, N. *India and the Commonwealth*, New Delhi, ABC Publishing House, 1983.

Judd, D. and Slinn, P. *The Evolution of the Modern Commonwealth*, London, Macmillan, 1982.

Mansergh, N. *The Commonwealth Experience*, vols 1 and 2, London, Weidenfeld & Nicolson, 1969.

Mehrotra, S.R. *India and the Commonwealth*, London, Allen & Unwin, 1965.

Miller, J.D.B. *Survey of Commonwealth Affairs, 1953–1969*, London, Oxford University Press, 1974.

Menzies, R.G. *Afternoon Light*, London, Cassell, 1967.

Nehru, J. *Letters to Chief Ministers*, vols 1 and 2, New Delhi, Teen Murti, 1986.

Nolutshungu, S.C. *Changing South Africa*, Manchester, Manchester University Press, 1982.

Payne, A.J. *The Politics of the Caribbean Community*, Manchester, Manchester University Press, 1980.

Ramphal, S.S. *One World to Share, Selected Speeches, 1975–1979*, London, Macmillan, 1979.

Sandys, D. *The Modern Commonwealth*, London, HMSO, 1962.

Smith, A., with Sanger, C. *Stitches in Time: The Commonwealth in World Politics*, London, André Deutsch, 1981.

Smith, T.E. *Commonwealth Migration, Flows and Policies*, London, Macmillan, 1981.

Tinker, H. *Experiment with Freedom: India and Pakistan, 1947*, London, Oxford Universtiy Press, 1967.

Tinker, H. *The Banyan Tree: Overseas Emigration from India, Pakistan and Bangladesh*, London, Oxford University Press, 1977.

Publications of the Commonwealth Secretariat
Reports of the Secretary-General, 1965–1987.
Commonwealth Heads of Government, Communiqués.
Reports of the Heads of Government Meetings.
The Commonwealth Today (issued in revised form every two years).

Periodicals
Choix, 'Francophonie et Commonwealth, Mythe ou réalités?', Quebec, Special Issue, 1978.
Commonwealth Today, London, World of Information.
Journal of Commonwealth and Comparative Politics, London, Institute of Commonwealth Studies.
Round Table, London, Butterworth.

For Product Safety Concerns and Information please contact our EU
representative GPSR@taylorandfrancis.com
Taylor & Francis Verlag GmbH, Kaufingerstraße 24, 80331 München, Germany

www.ingramcontent.com/pod-product-compliance
Lightning Source LLC
Chambersburg PA
CBHW071419290326
41932CB00046B/2476